Study Guide

to accompany

Nash • Jeffrey
Howe • Frederick • Davis • Winkler

THE AMERICAN PEOPLE
Creating a Nation and a Society

Volume One to 1865
Fourth Edition

Julie Roy Jeffrey
Goucher College

Peter J. Frederick
Wabash College

Neal A. Brooks
Essex Community College

Elizabeth M. Nix
Essex Community College

 LONGMAN

An Imprint of Addison Wesley Longman, Inc.

New York • Reading, Massachusetts • Menlo Park, California • Harlow, England
Don Mills, Ontario • Sydney • Mexico City • Madrid • Amsterdam

D1412097

Study Guide to accompany Nash/Jeffrey/Howe/Frederick/Davis/Winkler, *The American People: Creating a Nation and a Society*, Volume One, To 1865, Fourth Edition.

Copyright © 1998 Longman Publishers USA, a division of Addison Wesley Longman, Inc.

ISBN: 0-321-01634-3

CB

98 99 00 01 9 8 7 6 5 4 3 2

CONTENTS

"A people without history is like wind upon the buffalo grass."
—Lakota

Acknowledgments

Our ideas about teaching and learning have several sources, but none so important as those interactions and friendships with our students at Essex Community College and the University of Baltimore. From them we have learned to appreciate the trials and successes of students in an introductory history course. They have explained their dismay over the amount of material to read and digest, as well as the continual concern over which issues are most important. We thank our editors, Jessica Bayne and Jennifer McCaffery, at Addison Wesley Longman. Our colleague William C. Hughes has generously assisted with information from his extensive film data base. Special thanks are also due to Andrew Imparato for his editing and word processing skills, and to Susie Bane of Tech-Team in Timonium, Maryland, a former Essex student and talented word processor who assisted in the preparation of the fourth edition.

Neal A. Brooks/Elizabeth M. Nix

"The value of History is, indeed, not scientific but moral: by liberalizing the mind, by deepening the sympathies, by fortifying the will, it enables us to control, not society, but ourselves . . . and to meet the future."
—Carl L. Becker

INTRODUCTION

How to Do Well in Your History Course by Rediscovering the Past

In one of Garry Trudeau's "Doonesbury" cartoons, Mike and Zonker are strolling through the woods as Zonker reminisces about their college days. Among other things, he says, they went on study dates in the boat house, held midnight sledding parties, parked the dean's Volvo inside the chapel, got busted at a rock concert, and ran naked through a meeting of the board of trustees. After listening to Zonker's recollections of those "bright college years," Mike reminds him that "we never did any of those things." Zonker agrees, saying, "I know, but one day we'll think we did." "Isn't it a little early to start embellishing?" Mike asks. Zonker coolly responds, "You gotta grab the past while you can!" We introduce the Study Guide to *The American People: Creating a Nation and a Society* with this cartoon for two reasons. First, we are aware that the conflicting demands and pressures of college life often lead students to pranks, pizza parlors, parties, and paper deadline panics—the kinds of events that stimulated Zonker's imagination. Exaggerated and embellished as his fantasies were, they suggest the range of experiences we know students go through, or think about, during their college years. We certainly did. Our current fantasy is that you might add the study of American history to the positive college experiences that you will remember in later years—not made up, like Zonker's, but for real!

We have prepared this Study Guide, therefore, to smooth your way through the American history textbook, not as a substitute for it but as a supplement—a guide to reading *The American People* for maximum understanding, appreciation, enjoyment, and, yes, success on examinations. To be sure, you have many long hours of reading, reflection, and study ahead of you. Studying history is not easy. But it can be pleasurable as well as profitable, and we sincerely hope that you will find your study of American history almost as enjoyable—and certainly as educational—as the diversions that Zonker imagined as a college student.

We also introduce this Guide with Trudeau's cartoon because the last lines say something significant not only about students but also about historians. Although professionally committed to telling the truth about the past, which for the most part they succeed in doing, historians tend sometimes, like Zonker, to "embellish." Like any good storytellers, historians enjoy building an exciting drama by the addition of juicy adjectives and heightened tension. Occasionally they even get a date or name wrong. At one level this is inexcusable, and historians try to check and doublecheck their facts so as never to make errors. But they are only human, and both the authors of your textbook and your history professor may sometimes embellish or make mistakes. So will you, but your errors will be marked wrong. The ultimate responsibility for "getting the history right," therefore, is yours.

Historians also embellish when they interpret the past, not by telling inflated stories or committing factual errors but simply by showing their human point of view, which is the result of their particular time, place, circumstances, and personal backgrounds. Such factors influence the selection and interpretation of past events. Interpretation is unavoidable, and students should beware of a book or person that claims to be "the truth" rather than one interpretation of the truth.

All works of history, even textbooks, present a point of view reflecting the values, assumptions, and interests of the author. Interpretation differs from a biased presentation in that the latter willfully distorts truth while the former deepens understanding by the process of explaining how and why things happened in the past. This makes the writing (and teaching) of history more than a listing of names, dates, and other facts. The act of interpretation is a humble one, and you should be looking for the interpretive point of view of the authors of your textbook as you read. The Preface is a good place to start.

The history presented in *The American People* is enriched by an interpretive framework. It tells the story of the many ways in which the diverse people coming to this country—whether on foot across the Bering Straits, on rafts across the Rio Grande, or on the *Mayflower,* slave ships, or immigrant steamers—created a cultural mosaic of many societies, and one nation. These individual stories are the history, or "story," of "the American people." Our major goal is to help you both learn and enjoy this story. In the 1990s, as we continue to seek to know who we are by knowing where we came from, we realize that, like Michael Doonesbury, "you gotta grab the past while you can."

IMPORTANT ASSUMPTIONS TO BE AWARE OF

Toward that end, we have prepared this Study Guide. Your teacher has a similar one. We believe that you should know some of our most important assumptions as we prepared the textbook and these Guides. They are as follows:

1. The authors have tried to write a textbook that is not just a series of historical names, dates, places, and other facts — "one damned thing after another," as someone once described history. Rather, we show history as the story of the daily lives of both ordinary and famous Americans in the past. We have sought to take you inside these lives, to experience the fears, frustrations, and aspirations of the American people.

2. We want you not only to reexperience these lives but also to be confident that you remember what you have studied. When learning history is connected to your own experiences, as well as fun, you tend to do better on tests.

3. We believe that the textbook and Guides are only as good as they are teachable and learnable. We have designed both the text and these guides to be immediately usable, if an instructor desires, for a variety of classroom learning activities and assignments that enrich student learning and the appreciation of American history.

4. We believe that students become historians themselves the minute they open their textbooks and begin to read them. When you consulted your list of classes and other sources in order to discover what history course you signed up for and at what time and in what room it met, you were already acting as a historian, recovering a small piece of your own past in order to understand the present. We have designed a special feature in every chapter, called "Recovering the Past," to show the variety of ways in which <u>all</u> historians, including yourselves, work to construct the past.

5. We believe that students—all people, in fact—learn best when they begin with a personally compelling human experience, their own or someone else's. This human story suggests further stories, or facts, and some overarching themes and concepts. These are in turn analyzed, interpreted, compared to other facts, applied to other settings, and evaluated. Finally, there must be an opportunity to express what one has learned and to receive feedback on how well. We have structured the textbook and this Guide according to this basic pattern of human learning.

HOW TO UNDERSTAND A CHAPTER

Take Chapter 1, for example, which begins with the tragic story of Opechancanough, a Powhatan tribesman whose entire life of nearly 90 years was consumed by a struggle against the land hunger and alien values brought by Spanish and English newcomers to his ancestral lands in present-day Virginia near the Chesapeake Bay. After surviving germs brought by the Spanish and fighting many battles against English settlers near Jamestown, Opechancanough was captured and executed.

The brief anecdote about Opechancanough introduces most of the overarching themes and major concepts of Chapter 1: the intermingling in the North American wilderness of three worlds—red, white, and black—each with different life styles, cultural values, and aspirations. The result of this contact was terrible for the Native Americans, whether living in Spanish-controlled Central and South America or near English settlements in North America. Opechancanough's death at the hands of an English jailer in 1646 foreshadowed the destruction of Native Americans and their way of life by Europeans in coming centuries. Furthermore, the Spanish and English, though both white Europeans, were locked in combat with each other that had serious effects on the development of the Americas. In each chapter of the textbook, an anecdote of an ordinary person's life will, like the one about Opechancanough, suggest the major themes of the chapter. These themes are stated in the most important section of each chapter: the paragraphs that follow the opening story and precede the first main topic. Read these paragraphs very very carefully.

The bedrock of history, as many history students have found out to their despair, is composed of facts. Broad historical themes are the handles, or pegs, upon which to hang the many particular facts that make up the past. These facts must be mastered—often by memorization—in order to provide life and substance to the larger themes. In Chapter 1, for example, there are a number of names, dates, places, and terms. Once you are familiar with major concepts like the collision of three cultures and the disastrous outcome for Native Americans, these facts can be placed in some category, or hung on some peg, and are therefore easier to remember. Think, for example, of how you would remember the following facts: names such as Cortes, Elizabeth I, and Incas; dates such as "pre-Columbian," 1492, and 1607; places such as Peru, Venice, and Roanoke Island; and terms such as *matrilineal, the Reformation,* and *"the great dying."*

Once the facts are mastered within the context of the major themes, you are able to work with, or use, both facts and concepts in a more sophisticated way than just repeating or listing them. You could, for example, contrast the three worlds according to their differing values and beliefs about nature, religion, family, and political and economic goals. Or you could analyze the reasons for the conflict between Spain and England. Or you could apply or transfer your knowledge to similar situations, like the intermingling and conflicts today, perhaps even in your own community, among ethnic and racial groups with differing sets of values. Or you might evaluate how people thought and felt about the effects of the clash of cultures in both the seventeenth and twentieth centuries. Being able to form judgments like these is the highest level of learning and depends upon a prior understanding of specific facts and thematic concepts.

Finally, to check how well you have learned the material of a chapter, it is good to be tested—on both the specific facts and the larger themes of that chapter. This feedback is necessary both to confirm your confidence in how much has been learned and to identify areas that need further study.

To summarize, most people learn best by moving through the following sequence:

1. Engagement in a human story
2. An overview of major themes and concepts
3. Mastery of specific facts that support or illustrate those themes
4. Analysis, synthesis, comparison, application, and evaluation of the themes
5. An opportunity to demonstrate knowledge practicing these steps on tests and other assignments

Each chapter in *The American People* can be understood better by studying it in terms of this basic learning pattern.

HOW TO USE THE STUDY GUIDE WITH THE TEXT

The Study Guide also follows this pattern. Students who work back and forth from the chapter in *The American People* to the chapter in the Guide will continually be reinforcing and strengthening their mastery and enjoyment of American history. With a little experimenting, students will find that it is sometimes better to read the textbook chapter before looking at the Guide and sometimes better to read the Guide before the textbook.

We have also included PART summaries and the accounts of three important technological innovations to enhance your learning.

Each chapter contains the following sections:

(1) Chapter Outline (with opening anecdote)

It is helpful to look through the outline before reading a chapter in order to see at a glance both the major topics to be covered and the chapter's organization. The short summary of the human story or anecdote that begins each chapter should point toward these topics and suggest the structure.

(2) Significant Themes And Highlights

Three or four statements will provide an overview summary of the main themes, concepts, threads, major ideas, and special features of each chapter. To consult this section before reading the chapter may be the most helpful thing you can do in order to have some handles or pegs to help you understand and place the many particular facts encountered in the chapter. Keeping these major concepts in mind as you read will prevent you from getting lost in a sea of facts. Specific facts are valuable to a historian only as illustrations of some larger theme. If you have a strong sense of the themes you will more easily remember the appropriate illustrative factual examples when taking examinations.

(3) Learning Goals of the Chapter

The list of the goals, or objectives, of each chapter is a way of providing a self-check on how well you are mastering the material. After completing a chapter, try answering each item. If you can, you are ready to move on. If you cannot, you know which topics to review in the chapter. When you are preparing for examinations, reread the sections on learning goals for the appropriate chapters.

The first 5-6 learning goals indicate the "basic knowledge" you should be familiar with—the essential facts every history student has to know before doing anything else. Such knowledge is usually tested with short-answer exam questions: multiple-choice, true-or-false, identification, fill-in-the-blanks, and similar formats. You also need to know these facts in order to handle more difficult kinds of questions. The second part of the learning goals section includes three goals intended to give you "Practice in Historical Thinking Skills," higher order learning tasks such as analyzing, comparing and contrasting, applying, assessing, and evaluating historical phenomena. This is what we mean by interpretation. These intellectual skills are usually tested by essay questions and paper assignments. You can prepare for these by writing short practice essays on these three learning goals.

(4) Important Dates And Names to Know

Nothing drives history students crazier than having to memorize dates. Yet chronology—the order and sequence of past events—is essential to understanding history. What is most important for students to remember is not that they must memorize every exact date but rather that they should form a general idea of the sequence in which events happened. Remembering key dates is not as mysterious as students often think: it is usually just a matter of common sense. One could, for example, remember that the Declaration of Independence was signed in 1776 and the Constitution in 1787, but what is really important is to get them in the right order. Imagine how silly it would be to reverse them. It is common sense that the bonds of one government had to be dissolved before a new one could be created. The chronologies of important dates will usually include important names to remember as well. Names that are not associated with a particular date but are nevertheless significant are listed at the end of the chronology.

(5) Glossary of Important Terms

Although history is not nearly as filled with jargon and special vocabularies as other disciplines, various unfamiliar terms inevitably turn up in every chapter. These are listed and briefly identified in this section. Remember that your teachers may also have favorite terms that they want you to learn, so it is a good idea to add them to these lists.

(6) Enrichment Ideas

We think this is the most important section in the Guides. In this part is a list of activities and assignments designed to aid and enhance learning of the important themes and concepts in each chapter. Some are activities you can follow and do on your own. A longer list, not included in the Student Guide, contains assignments and classroom activities your instructor may want to use. The variety of suggested approaches to enrich learning—both in the classroom and out—is extensive, but they always begin with further ways of using the "Recovering the Past" feature. This section, found in each chapter, is intended to introduce students of history to the many sources and ways in which historians find out what happened in the past.

A century ago, most historians would probably have said that they recovered the past by reading old manuscripts, primarily government and other institutional documents housed in official archives, and by consulting the letters, papers, and manuscripts of former presidents, senators, generals, and other leaders. But in recent years, as historians have broadened their interest from political and military history (unkindly called "drum and trumpets" history) to include the social history of ordinary people, they have also widened the kinds of sources they find useful in recovering the past. To written government documents and archival manuscripts historians have added private diaries, popular songs, paintings, cartoons, census returns, tax and inventory lists, films and photographs, material objects, oral history, and many other means of recovering the past.

The "RTPs," as the authors affectionately call them, are intended not only to enrich your learning of American history but also to show you how you can become your own historian. For the most part, each means of recovering the past is appropriate to the content of the chapter in which it is found. Thus the work of archaeologists and the contributions archaeology makes to understanding earlier civilizations are discussed in Chapter 1; folktales in the chapter on slavery; and films, oral history, and television in the twentieth-century chapters. Additional ways of recovering the past, such as popular Hollywood feature films and trips to historical areas, are mentioned in the appropriate Enrichment sections in this Study Guide.

(7) Sample Test And Examination Questions

Many students will find this section most useful in preparing for examinations, not because their teachers will necessarily select test questions from those included (though they might) but because students can check for themselves how well they have learned the material in a chapter. Note that the sample questions begin with short-answer types (multiple choice, matching, etc.) to test basic knowledge (how well you remember the material), whereas the later questions are essays and interpretive questions that test historical thinking skills (how well you can compare and contrast, analyze, interpret, apply, and evaluate the main ideas of the chapter). In these higher order questions, you gain practice in learning how to think like historians, doing the kind of basic detective groundwork interpreting evidence from various sources and writing analytic essays.

The test questions for some chapters in this Guide end with a map question, which is a lower-order but fundamentally important content knowledge skill (knowing where places are). Other chapters end with a quotation, chart, or other verbal or quantitative illustration, which we ask you to identify and interpret—who, what, where, when, and why significant. This is a more sophisticated exercise in the detection and interpretation of a historical source.

HOW TO UNDERLINE A CHAPTER

One of the first problems students face when they begin reading a textbook is how much to underline or highlight. A consideration of the purpose of underlining may help guide you through a chapter. The major goal, of course, is to aid memory and comprehension by highlighting the main themes, selecting important examples for each major idea. This helps not only to understand the chapter but also to review for examinations. Too little underlining means that you may end up rereading the entire chapter the night before a test. Too much, in which no discrimination has taken place, may also mean having to reread everything. It is, of course, important to note the topic sentences for each paragraph.

The following is an example of how we would underline a short section from Chapter 1.

Contrasting World Views

Colonizing Europeans called themselves "civilized" and typically described the people they met in the Americas as "savage," "heathen," or "barbarian." But the <u>gulf separating people in Europe and North America</u> was not defined so much by how the <u>two cultures</u> extracted a food supply from the land, housed themselves, or organized family life as by <u>how they viewed their relationship to the environment and defined social relations in their communities</u>. In these areas, a <u>wide difference in values existed</u>. This created the potential for a dangerous conflict once the Atlantic Ocean that had separated two ancient civilizations had been transformed from a barrier to a bridge by a technological and scientific leap forward by western Europeans in the fifteenth century.

In the <u>view of Europeans the natural world was a resource designed for man's use</u>. "Subdue the earth," read the first book of the Old Testament, "and have dominion over every living thing that moves on the earth." God ruled the cosmos, bringing floods, droughts, and earthquakes, but humans could reshape their physical surroundings into a productive and secure world. Man's relationship to the natural environment was a secular matter, even if God, in the sacred sphere, sometimes intervened.

<u>Native Americans,</u> in contrast, were "<u>a people that are contented with Nature as they find her</u>," as one colonist phrased it. In their ethos, <u>every part of the natural environment was sacred</u>. Rocks, trees, and animals <u>all possessed spiritual power</u>, and all were linked to form a sacred whole. To injure the environment, by overfishing or abusing it in any way, was to offend the spiritual power present throughout nature and hence to risk spiritual retaliation. In the villages of Europe, peasant people had similarly believed in spirits residing in trees and rocks, but such "superstition" was fading.

Regarding the soil as a resource to be exploited for man's benefit, <u>Europeans</u> believed that <u>land should be privately possessed</u>. <u>Individual ownership of property became a fundamental concept</u>, and an extensive institutional apparatus grew up to support it. <u>Fences</u> symbolized private property, <u>inheritance</u> became the mechanism for transmitting land from one generation to another within the same family, and courts gained the power to settle property disputes. <u>Property</u> was the <u>basis</u> not only of sustenance but also of <u>independence</u>, <u>material wealth</u>, <u>political status</u>, and personal identity. The social structure directly mirrored patterns of land ownership, with a land-wealthy elite at the apex of the social pyramid and a mass of propertyless individuals forming the broad base.

<u>Native Americans</u> also had concepts of property, and tribes recognized territorial boundaries. But they believed that <u>land was invested with sacred qualities and should be held in common</u>. As one German missionary to the Delaware Indians explained their view in the eighteenth century, the Creator "made the Earth and all that it contains for the <u>common good of mankind</u>. Whatever liveth on the land, whatsoever groweth out of the earth, and all that is in the rivers and waters . . . was given jointly to all and everyone is entitled to his share."

<u>Communal ownership sharply limited social stratification in most tribal communities</u>. Accustomed to wide disparities of wealth, Europeans often found this remarkable. Observing the Iroquois of the eastern woodlands in 1657, a French Jesuit noted with surprise that they had no almshouses because "their kindness, humanity and courtesy not only makes them liberal with what they have, but causes them to possess hardly anything except in common. A whole village must be without corn, before any individual can be obliged to endure privation." Not all Europeans were acquisitive, competitive individuals. The majority were peasants scratching a subsistence living from the soil, living in kin-centered villages with little contact with the outside world, and exchanging goods and labor through barter. <u>But in Europe's urban centers a wealth-conscious, striving individual</u> who celebrated wider choices and greater opportunities to enhance personal status was coming to the fore. In contrast, <u>Native American traditions stressed the group rather than the individual</u>. Holding land and other resources in common, Indian societies were usually more egalitarian and their members more concerned with personal valor than personal wealth.

<u>Exceptions</u> to this cultural system occurred in the highly developed and populous Aztec and Inca empires and, in North America, among a few tribes such as the Natchez. But on the eastern and western coasts of the continent and in the Southwest—the regions of contact in the sixteenth and seventeenth centuries—the European newcomers encountered a people whose cultural values differed strikingly from theirs.

European colonizers in North America also found disturbing the <u>matrilineal organization of many tribal societies</u>. <u>Contrary to European practice</u>, family membership among the Iroquois, for example, was determined through the female line.

A COLONIZING PEOPLE
1492 - 1776

America has always been a nation of immigrants, an elaborate cultural mosaic created out of the unending streams of people who for four centuries have flocked to its shores from every corner of the world. It is the colonial roots of this intermingling of people and cultures that provide an organizing framework for the first part of this book. America began with the convergence of people from the three continents of North America, Europe, and Africa. We examine the mingling of their values, institutions, and lifeways during the fifteenth and sixteenth centuries in Chapter 1, "Three Worlds Meet." Chapter 2, "Colonizing a Continent," explores five regions of settlement along the Atlantic seaboard. The interplay of religious idealism, economic opportunity, political experimentation, and social adaptation to the new environment is examined on the Chesapeake tobacco coast; in Puritan New England; in the French, Dutch, and English colonies from the St. Lawrence to the Hudson rivers; in proprietary Carolina; and in Quaker Pennsylvania.

The ability to grow from small and struggling settlements in the seventeenth century to thriving, more populous colonies in the early eighteenth century depended above all on exploiting the natural resources of North America. Chapter 3, "Mastering the New World," explores how colonists struggled against Native Americans to expand their land base and turned to slave labor in the southern colonies. While controlling Native Americans and African slaves, the colonists also had to master themselves as social and political tensions grew at the end of the seventeenth century. At the same time, French ambitions in North America challenged the territorial mastery of England's American colonies and involved them in another kind of conflict.

Chapter 4, "The Maturing of Colonial Society," traces the development of the colonies of England, Spain, and France in the first half of the eighteenth century. It stresses the increasingly complex yet unfinished character of colonial society, highlights its regional differences, and shows how economic growth, religious revival, and political maturation prepared the English colonists by 1750 for the epic events that would occur in the next generation. It was this fluidity of colonial society that made the Seven Years' War (1756-1763) and the subsequent coming of the American Revolution such a multifaceted and dynamic period, as Chapter 5, "Bursting the Colonial Bonds," spells out. Many other "American revolutions" will follow in our history.

1

Three Worlds Meet

(1) CHAPTER OUTLINE

For his entire life of 90 years in the Chesapeake Bay region, the Powhatan tribesman Opechancanough struggled to defend his land and way of life against the intrusions of the Spanish and English (and even Africans), thus showing how the lives of red, white, and black people were intertwined in North America.

The People of America Before Columbus
> Hunters and Farmers
> Native Americans in 1600
> Contrasting World Views

Africa on the Eve of Contact
> The Kingdoms of Africa
> The African Ethos

Europe in the Age of Exploration
> The Rise of Europe
> The New Monarchies and the Expansionist Impulse
> Reaching the Americas
> Religious Conflict During the Reformation

The Iberian Conquest of America
> The Spanish Juggernaut
> The Great Dying
> Silver, Sugar, and Their Consequences
> Spain's Northern Frontier

England Looks West
> England Challenges Spain
> The Westward Fever
> Anticipating North America

Conclusion: Converging Worlds

(2) SIGNIFICANT THEMES AND HIGHLIGHTS

1. The clash of three cultures from three continents—North America, Europe, and Africa—forms the opening chapter of American history and is therefore the opening chapter of the textbook. With Opechancanough's life story we see the collision and intermingling of three worlds—red, white, and black. The converging of cultural values and aspirations, often accompanied by violence and disease, disrupted and nearly destroyed the red world, enslaved the victims from the black world, and furthered the expansion and development of the white world.

2. A secondary clash within the European white world, that between Catholic Spain and Protestant England, explains the different development of Spanish Central and South America and English North America.

3. By taking readers inside the cultural beliefs and experiences of Native Americans and Africans, as well as Europeans, this chapter serves to counteract the traditional ethnocentric view that sees all developments through the eyes of Europeans. An example of this is the oft-repeated phrase "Columbus discovered America," implying that there was no life or culture in the Americas until a European found it in 1492.

(3) LEARNING GOALS

Familiarity with Basic Knowledge

After reading this chapter, you should be able to:

1. Locate and briefly describe the Native American Mound Builders of the Ohio and Mississippi river valleys, the Pueblo dwellers of the Southwest, and the woodland Indians of the East Coast.

2. Describe Native American attitudes toward and beliefs about the natural world, wealth, community, family, and men and women.

3. Name and locate three West African kingdoms between the fifth and fourteenth centuries and describe West African beliefs about family, religion, and social organization.

4. Explain the political, economic, and religious changes in early modern Europe that led to the exploration and eventual settlement of North America.

5. Locate on a map the names and routes of the most significant Iberian, English, French, and Dutch explorers and conquerors in the fifteenth and sixteenth centuries.

6. Describe the impact of the European conquest of the Americas on the Native American Indian population.

Practice in Historical Thinking Skills

After reading this chapter, you should be able to:

1. Compare and contrast the values and lifestyles of the three worlds—red, white, and black—that met in the Americas early in the sixteenth century.

2. Evaluate the outcomes of that collision for each world. What do you think and feel about these outcomes?

3. Compare and contrast the cultures of Spain and England, and their motivations for settling the Americas.

(4) IMPORTANT DATES AND NAMES TO KNOW

Pre-Columbian epochs:

12,000 B.C.	Beringian epoch ends
6,000 B.C.	Paleo-Indian phase ends
500 B.C.	Archaic era ends
500 B.C.-A.D. 1500	Post-Archaic era in North America Kingdoms of Ghana, Mali, Songhay, and Benin in Africa
c.1000	Norse seafarers establish settlements in Newfoundland
1420s-1480s	Portuguese sailors explore west coast of Africa
1469	Marriage of Ferdinand and Isabella
1492	Christopher Columbus lands on Caribbean islands Spanish expel Moors (Muslims) and Jews
1494	Treaty of Tordesillas
1497-1585	French and British explore northern part of the Americas
1498	Vasco da Gama reaches India after sailing around Africa
1513	Portuguese explorers reach China
1515-1565	Spanish explore Florida and southern parts of North America
1520s	Luther attacks Catholicism
1521	Cortés captures Mexico City, conquering the Aztecs

1530s	Calvin calls for religious reform
1533	Pizarro captures Cuzco, conquering the Incas
1515-1565	Spanish explore Florida and southern part of North America
1540-1542	Coronado explores the Southwest
1558	Elizabeth I crowned queen of England
1585	Roanoke Island settlement
1588	English defeat the Spanish Armada
1603	James I succeeds Elizabeth I
1607	English begin settlement at Jamestown, Virginia
1608	French settlement begins in Quebec

Other Names to Know

Prince Henry the Navigator	Jacques Cartier	John Cabot
Hernando de Soto	Richard Hakluyt	Giovanni da Verrazano
	Ponce de Leon	Cahokia

(5) GLOSSARY OF IMPORTANT TERMS

Pre-Columbian era: the period of history before Columbus in which Native American Indian cultures lived in the Americas undiscovered—and unaffected—by Europeans

matrilineal: tracing descent and property and political rights through the mother

Renaissance: period of cultural rebirth in Europe (fifteenth-sixteenth centuries)

Protestant Reformation: period in Europe in the sixteenth century of protest against the Roman Catholic church and the creation of new (Protestant) religious institutions

Muslim: a person believing in the religion of Islam, which began in the seventh century and spread throughout the Middle East and northern Africa and eventually to Asia and Europe in succeeding centuries (Muslims, or Moslems, were sometimes called Moors by Europeans)

(6) ENRICHMENT IDEAS

1. Find out which Native American tribes and nations lived in your part of the country and whether there are any archaeological working sites or remains, like Cahokia, to visit. Also visit any museums or historical parks that feature local Indian history.

2. Assume that you are an archaeologist or anthropologist who wants to understand and reconstruct in your region as much of the original Indian culture and typical daily life as possible from relics and other remains. Present your findings to others in various forms: oral report, written paper, table display showing artifacts and a model of Indian life, or artistic drawings or skits illustrating Indian culture.

3. Pretend that you are an archaeologist or anthropologist from some distant future who wants to understand and reconstruct as much as possible of present-day culture and daily life in your community. Imagine the absolute destruction of all written records and the near-destruction and burying under dirt and debris of material objects and structures. As you dig up the remains or observe unusual topological and other features (like dammed-up streams, terraced and flattened hills, or roadway patterns), how much of the original daily life and culture do you think you could reconstruct?

4. Imagine yourself as an alien, who has never seen earthlings, arriving to explore and settle the planet Earth. From the behavior of human beings what kind of conclusions might you draw about their cultural patterns and values? What images do you have about groups different from your own? Think about both positive and negative images.

5. Look over the opening anecdote. Imagine yourself as Opechancanough going through the various epochs of his life. Write a speech or memoir on what he might have thought about the values and cultural norms of white people in the different seasons of his life.

(7) SAMPLE TEST AND EXAMINATION QUESTIONS

Multiple choice: Choose the best answer.

1. The "New World" was first entered by people from the "Old World"
   a. about 12,000 to 28,000 years ago
   b. about 5,000 to 10,000 years ago
   c. in about A.D.1000
   d. in 1492

2. The greatest loss of life for Native Americans during the sixteenth and seventeenth centuries was caused by
   a. intertribal warfare
   b. intermarriage with Europeans
   c. conversion to European religions
   d. infectious disease brought by Europeans

3. Cahokia was the center of
   a. "Hopewell" culture
   b. "Mississippi" culture
   c. "Pueblo" culture
   d. "Iroquois" culture

4. According to Native Americans, before the European invasion
   a. the natural world was a resource given by a Christian God
   b. every part of the natural environment was sacred
   c. the belief that spirits resided in nature was fading
   d. land was the basis of status and identity

5. From the fifth to the fourteenth centuries, West Africa
   a. was a savage land of nomadic hunters
   b. was colonized and exploited by various European nations
   c. was engaged in perpetual warfare with Muslims from the Middle East
   d. featured the development of a series of kingdoms with relatively advanced cultures and complex political structures

6. In the fifteenth century, West African societies
   a. developed an extensive industrial system based on slaves captured in tribal wars
   b. had the most brutal system of slavery in the civilized world
   c. respected the privileges of education and marriage and the protection of the law for slaves
   d. provided legal protection and rights only for slave children

7. By the fifteenth and sixteenth centuries a new political entity, _____, had arisen in Europe.
   a. dictatorships
   b. democracies
   c. feudal states
   d. nation-states

8. All of the following changes in fifteenth-century Europe led to an expansionist impulse EXCEPT
   a. the rise of new monarchies
   b. the rise of Calvinism
   c. technological improvements
   d. trade rivalry with the Muslims

9. According to Martin Luther,
   a. only a chosen few deserved salvation
   b. only non-Catholics could ever be saved
   c. salvation came through faith in God's grace
   d. salvation was earned through good works

10. The Treaty of Tordesillas divided settlement of the Americas between
    a. Spain and Portugal
    b. Spain and England
    c. Spain and France
    d. France and England

11. What percentage (estimated) of the inhabitants of the Americas died of diseases brought by the Europeans?
    a. 20 percent
    b. 40 percent
    c. 65 percent
    d. 90 percent

12. Which of the following best describes England's motivations for moving westward to North America?
    a. the quest for new fisheries
    b. the quest for gold and silver
    c. religious and trading rivalry with Spain
    d. the desire to Christianize heathen Indians

13. Which of the following pairs is not correct?
    a. Pizarro - Incas
    b. Cortés - Aztecs
    c. de Soto - New Mexico and Arizona
    d. Ponce de Leon - Florida

14. Early European images of the "New World"
    a. described an earthly paradise full of riches
    b. depicted friendly native inhabitants
    c. pictured backward, hostile savages
    d. described all of the above

15. Columbus was responsible for
    a. giving Spain an opportunity to develop and exploit the resources of the Americas
    b. finding a new water route to India
    c. the first sea voyage around Cape Horn
    d. discovering that the world was round

Essays

1. Compare and contrast Native American and European beliefs and practices about the natural world, property and wealth, and community and family life.

2. Analyze English motivations for exploring and eventually settling the New World.

3. Evaluate the converging of three worlds—red, black, and white—in the Americas. What was gained and what was lost by each of the three?

4. "Neither the Spanish nor the English respected Indian culture and society; this lack of respect enabled them to destroy Native American life with few regrets." Write an essay supporting this statement, selecting appropriate evidence.

5. Explain how the religious changes of the Protestant Reformation affected the English colonization of America.

2

Colonizing a Continent

(1) CHAPTER OUTLINE

Captain John Mason leaves the Massachusetts Bay Colony with other Puritans in search of better lands. They establish the new community of Windsor on the Connecticut River. Shortly afterward, Mason leads hundreds of the settlers in an attack on the Pequot Indians, massacring them.

The Chesapeake Tobacco Coast
    Jamestown
    Sot Weed and Indentured Servants
    Expansion and Indian War
    Proprietary Maryland
    Daily Life on the Chesapeake

Massachusetts and Its Offspring
    Puritanism in England
    Puritan Predecessors in New England
    Errand into the Wilderness
    An Elusive Utopia
    New Englanders and Indians
    The Web of Village Life

From the St. Lawrence to the Hudson
    England Challenges the Mighty Dutch

Proprietary Carolina: A Restoration Reward
    The Indian Debacle
    Early Carolina Society

The Quakers' Peaceable Kingdom
    The Early Friends
    Early Quaker Designs
    Pacifism in a Militant World: Quakers and Indians
    Building the Peaceable Kingdom
    The Limits of Perfectionism

Conclusion: The Achievement of New Societies

(2) SIGNIFICANT THEMES AND HIGHLIGHTS

1. A theme running throughout the chapter, illustrated by the Pequot massacre, is the confrontation in North America between two cultures: the English colonists (in various kinds of settlements) and the Native American Indians. The two cultures collided as the colonists sought to realize the goals that had lured them to the New World and the Indians sought to defend their tribal homelands.

2. A second theme focuses on tensions growing out of the religious and economic motivations behind settlement. Many English colonists came to America to create religious utopias, a New World Zion. Others, even in the same settlement, came for economic opportunity, gold, and land. Regardless of motive, the colonists experienced limits to their aspirations: both utopia and economic opportunity proved elusive, the former far more than the latter.

3. Another recurrent theme of the chapter is the tension between religious idealism and violence. The colonial world was a violent one, both in contact with the Native Americans and in the social conflicts that emerged in the difficult early years of settlement.

4. The English colonists not only clashed with Native American cultures but also developed different cultures themselves. This chapter is structured around the reconstruction of the modes of settlement and character of life in five distinctly different societies along the Atlantic Coast: the Chesapeake region of Virginia and Maryland, Puritan New England, New York under the Dutch and English, proprietary Carolina, and Quaker Pennsylvania. In the account of each society is a picture of daily life as reflected in the architecture of houses, material household belongings, patterns of family life, and the role of women.

(3) LEARNING GOALS

Familiarity with Basic Knowledge

After reading this chapter, you should be able to:

1. Locate the various distinct settlements on a map of the Atlantic Coast, in particular Jamestown and the Chesapeake Bay tobacco area, Roanoke Island, Charleston, Plymouth, Boston and Massachusetts Bay, New York, the Hudson River, Delaware, the Connecticut and James rivers, and Philadelphia and the greater Pennsylvania settlement.

2. Describe the changing population, social patterns, and daily life of the Chesapeake tobacco coast in the seventeenth century.

3. Describe the beliefs, social patterns, and character of village life of the New England Puritans in England in early seventeenth-century Massachusetts.

4. Outline the major features of economic and social life in seventeenth-century New York and Carolina.

5. Describe Quaker beliefs and the efforts to build a peaceable kingdom in William Penn's settlement in Pennsylvania.

Practice in Historical Thinking Skills

After reading this chapter, you should be able to:

1. Compare and contrast the reasons and motivations for the settlement of each of the five main colonies, and describe the relationship of each of the five settlements with the Native American Indians of that region.

2. Reconstruct and compare the essentials of daily life, including the lives of women, in each of the five settlements in the seventeenth century.

3. Discuss whether you think utopian idealism or economic necessity was a more important motivation in the settlement and development of the English colonies.

(4) IMPORTANT DATES AND NAMES TO KNOW

1590	Roanoke Island colony fails
1604-1609	Samuel de Champlain establishes fur trading stations in French Canada
1607	Jamestown settled
1616-1621	Native American population in New England devastated by European diseases
1617	First tobacco crop shipped from Virginia
1619	First Africans arrive in Jamestown (Virginia)
1620	Pilgrims land at Plymouth (Massachusetts)
1622	Powhatan tribes attack Virginia settlements
1624	Dutch colonize mouth of Hudson River (New Netherland)
1630	Puritan migration to Massachusetts Bay

1632	Maryland grant to Lord Baltimore (George Calvert)
1633-1634	Native Americans in New England again struck by European diseases
1635	Roger Williams banished to Rhode Island
1636	Anne Hutchinson exiled to Rhode Island
1637	New England wages war against the Pequot Indians
1642-1649	English Civil War ends great migration to New England
1643	Confederation of New England
1659-1661	Four Quakers hanged on Boston Common
1660	Restoration of King Charles II
1663	Carolina charter granted to eight proprietors
1664	English capture New Netherland and rename it New York Royal grant of the Jersey lands to proprietors
1680	Popé's revolt in New Mexico
1681	William Penn receives Pennsylvania grant

Other Names to Know

Captain John Smith	Opechancanough
Powhatan	William Bradford
John Winthrop	George Fox

(5) GLOSSARY OF IMPORTANT TERMS

indentured servants: European migrants, usually young and single, who entered into work contracts for a specified period of years in exchange for free passage to the New World and sometimes a promise of land at the end of the contract

proprietors: prominent Englishmen to whom the king granted vast areas of land in the New World

antinomianism: an interpretation of Puritan doctrine associated with Anne Hutchinson that stressed mystical elements in God's grace and diverged from orthodox Puritan views on salvation

Puritans: English Protestants who wished not only to purify the Church of England but also to reform English society; they came to New England to set up a model community as an example to England

Pilgrims: a radical separatist group of English Protestants who settled at Plymouth in order to be left alone to lead a pure and primitive life

Society of Friends (Quakers): a visionary radical sect, much persecuted, whose members believed in, among other things, an inner light that brought them close to God, equality in religious and social life, pacifism, and defiance of authority when it denied their right to practice their religion

magistrates: secular, civil leaders in Massachusetts Bay, usually not ministers

(6) ENRICHMENT IDEAS

1. As an extension of the Recovering the Past section in this chapter, recall the differences in housing between Massachusetts Bay and the Chesapeake region. How do the houses and their furnishings show the differences and similarities in the two societies? Find examples of house design in Maryland and Virginia in the early eighteenth century. What are the significant differences between the earlier Chesapeake housing and these? What do the newer designs reveal about social and economic changes? You can also compare the Boardman house to eighteenth-century Massachusetts houses to see what kind of changes have taken place there.

2. As a class project, make replicas or plans of typical villages from each settlement. This can include everything from designs on paper to miniature villages on tabletops fashioned out of balsa wood/craft wood sticks and the like. Note how house designs reflect daily life in the different settlements.

3. Write a letter or diary entry describing the daily life of a typical inhabitant on a typical day in three of the five settlements in seventeenth-century America.

4. Construct an imaginary document reflecting each settlement's attitude toward and relationship with the area's Indian tribes. The document might be a sermon, a treaty, a leader's policy statement, a letter by a young man or woman in the settlement, or a speech (or letter) by a young Indian of the appropriate area.

5. Imagine yourself to be an indentured servant in the Chesapeake. Were you to write a letter home to a brother or sister, how would you describe your life? Would you encourage your brother or sister to come to the New World?

6. For those near local museums with eighteenth century exhibits, a visit and brief description of items and their significance will enhance understanding of daily life.

(7) SAMPLE TEST AND EXAMINATION QUESTIONS

Multiple choice: Choose the best answer.

1. The Jamestown colony suffered all of the following problems of population EXCEPT
    a. too few skilled workers
    b. too many gold-seeking gentlemen
    c. too many slaves
    d. too few women

2. Most indentured servants who came to Virginia and Maryland in the seventeenth century were
    a. married couples
    b. young, single, and male
    c. young, single, and female
    d. black Africans

3. Houses in the Chesapeake region were
    a. crude, one-room structures
    b. large homes with sleeping lofts and lean-to kitchens
    c. small predecessors of plantation-style houses
    d. connected to long, tobacco-drying barns

4. Women in Chesapeake society, as compared to New England,
    a. died young and were scarce
    b. were given religious freedom
    c. lived long lives, bearing many children
    d. were at the center of both economic and political life

5. Puritans migrated to Massachusetts Bay because they wanted
    a. to convert heathens
    b. religious liberty and purity
    c. to set up an experiment in religious toleration
    d. to be left alone to pursue their vision of a pure religious community

6. Which colony is not matched with its major crop?
    a. Virginia-tobacco
    b. South Carolina-rice
    c. West Indies-bananas
    d. Massachusetts-fish

7. The massacre at Jamestown in 1622
    a. avenged the Pequot massacre in Connecticut
    b. was used as justification by many to make permanent war on the Indians
    c. virtually wiped out the entire English colony
    d. was led by a disappointed Powhatan suitor of Pocahontas

8. Roger Williams was a problem for the ruling authorities in Massachusetts Bay primarily because
   a. he advocated the separation of church and state
   b. he accused the Puritans of illegal intrusion on Indian lands
   c. he was too pure and godly
   d. all of the above

9. Anne Hutchinson was excommunicated from a Boston church primarily because
   a. she preached numerous erroneous theological opinions
   b. she incited wives to demand equal rights from their husbands
   c. she opposed wage and price controls
   d. all of the above

10. New England women
    a. played a significant role in deciding church policies
    b. died in childbirth at a younger age than European women
    c. lived longer but bore fewer children than the European norm
    d. played a significant role in the family-centered society

11. Which is the correct order of settlement?
    a. Carolina, Pennsylvania, Maryland, Rhode Island
    b. Rhode Island, Pennsylvania, Maryland, Carolina
    c. Rhode Island, Maryland, Carolina, Pennsylvania
    d. Maryland, Carolina, Rhode Island, Pennsylvania

12. Quakers believed in all of the following EXCEPT
    a. equality of all persons, including women, in religious matters
    b. renunciation of the use of force in human affairs
    c. renunciation of making money as an affront to God
    d. no church leaders or institutions standing between an individual and God

13. The most harmonious relations between English colonists and Native American Indians were found in
    a. Pennsylvania
    b. Carolina
    c. Massachusetts Bay
    d. Virginia

14. The pattern of the Quaker dispersal into rural Pennsylvania was to settle
    a. in compact towns, as in New England
    b. in closely knit Quaker kinship groups from the same European regions
    c. in large towns populated by diverse nationality groups
    d. as individual families, thus fracturing a sense of identity and community

15. According to the chapter author, the foundations for pluralism in America were laid in
   a. the Massachusetts pattern of settling new towns
   b. Penn's policies of peaceful relations with the Indians
   c. Penn's policies of toleration and open immigration
   d. the diversity represented by the different settlements along the Atlantic Coast

Identify and show a relationship between each of the following pairs:

Virginia	*and*	Massachusetts Bay Company
meetinghouse	*and*	town meeting
Captain John Smith	*and*	Powhatan
Captain John Mason	*and*	Roger Williams
George Fox	*and*	Mary Dyer
John Winthrop	*and*	William Bradford
William Penn	*and*	New Netherland

[This question form, which invites a short essay, combines a basic memory task (identifying the person or term) with a higher-order thinking skill (showing a connection). Note that the instruction says "a" relationship, not "the" relationship, suggesting that there is no single "right answer." There are many possible connections, but in the following example each new answer is better than the last: Captain Mason and Roger Williams were "both Puritans"; they were both Puritans who left Massachusetts Bay to start other colonies; they were both Puritans who left Massachusetts Bay for different reasons, one willingly and the other banished; they were both Puritans who left Massachusetts Bay to found new colonies and who had different attitudes toward the Indians—Mason massacred them and Williams befriended them.]

Essays

1. Compare and contrast the social patterns of life in the Chesapeake area, New England, and Pennsylvania.

2. The character of immigration to the Chesapeake, Massachusetts Bay, the Carolinas, and Pennsylvania goes a long way toward explaining the social development of each place. Discuss with evidence.

3. Why do you think utopian perfectionism proved to be so elusive for colonial Americans? To what extent do you think the answer is found in human nature or in historical conditions?

Identify and Interpret: Quotation
(that is, state who, what, where, when, and why significant)

We must be knit together in this work as one man. We must entertain each other in brotherly affection. . . . We must delight in each other, make others' conditions our own, rejoice together, mourn together, labor and suffer together: always having before our eyes our commission and community in the work, our community as members of the same body. . . . We shall find that the God of Israel is among us, when ten of us shall be able to resist a thousand of our enemies, when He shall make us a praise and glory, that men shall say of succeeding plantations: "The Lord make it like that of New England." For we must consider that we shall be as a city upon a hill, the eyes of all people are upon us.

3

Mastering the New World

(1) CHAPTER OUTLINE

Anthony and Mary Johnson, two freed slaves, live in the uneasy world between freedom and slavery. Although the family initially prospers, as attitudes toward blacks harden they find fewer and fewer opportunities available to them. The Johnson children and grandchildren are unable to match the modest success of Anthony and Mary.

African Bondage
    The Slave Trade
    The Southern Transition to Black Labor
    Slavery in the Northern Colonies
    The System of Bondage

Slave Culture
    The Growth of Slavery
    Resistance and Rebellion
    Black Religion and Family

The Struggle for Land
    King Philip's War in New England
    Bacon's Rebellion Engulfs Virginia

An Era of Instability
    Organizing the Empire
    The Glorious Revolution in New England
    Leisler's Rebellion in New York
    Southern Rumblings
    The Social Basis of Politics
    Witchcraft in Salem

Contending for a Continent
    Anglo-French Rivalry
    The Results of War

Conclusion: Controlling the New Environment

(2) SIGNIFICANT THEMES AND HIGHLIGHTS

1. This chapter treats five conflicts in the colonial period between 1675 and 1715: two dealt with the European colonial effort to establish mastery over African slaves and Native American Indians; two concerned administrative and class struggles among the English colonists themselves; the final one was an international struggle as the British sought mastery over French, Dutch, and Spanish colonial contenders.

2. Although the boundaries of American slavery were at first fluid, as the Johnsons' experience showed, the institution of slavery altered the shape of American society. Slavery became a primary source of labor and profits in the Chesapeake region but was also closely bound up with economic life in the North. Slavery profoundly affected the lives of both white and black Americans and was an ironic comment on the dream of America as a place of refuge and hope. The personal stories of Olaudah Equiano and the Johnson clan convey some of the pain connected with slavery and the status of blacks.

3. At the same time that racial boundaries between blacks and whites were hardening, the violent battle of whites for Native American lands continued. The struggle is described in New England, the Chesapeake region, and South Carolina. Although losses were heavy for both Native Americans and white settlers, in the end the coastal tribes were defeated.

4. Small insurrections against colonial administrators and elites, triggered by the Glorious Revolution of 1688, erupted in several colonies. Although they were in no way a "dress rehearsal" for the American Revolution, they did reveal some of the social and political tensions growing out of the attempt to plant English society in the New World.

5. Soon after these insurrections, Europe plunged into war. Rivalries of the Old World affected the New even though the major battlefields were, in fact, far away from the colonies. The impact of European events on the colonies is another indication of the close bonds between the new society and the old.

(3) LEARNING GOALS

Familiarity with Basic Knowledge

After reading this chapter, you should be able to:

1. Describe the slave trade and explain three ways in which the presence of black slaves altered the direction of American society.

2. Give three reasons for the transformation of the Chesapeake labor force in the late seventeenth century.

3. Describe cultural features of African-Americans in the seventeenth century.

4. Describe the course and consequences of King Philip's War in New England and Bacon's Rebellion in Virginia.

5. Explain the key ideas England used to organize her empire. How was control affected by the Glorious Revolution?

6. State three basic differences between the French and English settlements in North America. Why did France and England compete for control of North America?

Practice in Historical Thinking Skills

After reading this chapter, you should be able to:

1. Analyze how the conflicts between Englishmen and Africans and Native Americans, among Englishmen themselves, and between the British and other European nations changed the relations among white, black, and red people in the New World.

2. Show the most important effects of the Glorious Revolution in England and of European national rivalries on the colonies in the late seventeenth and early eighteenth centuries.

3. Explain why the late seventeenth century has been described as a period of great instability and change in American history.

(4) IMPORTANT DATES AND NAMES TO KNOW

1600-1700	Dutch monopolize slave trade
1619	First Africans imported to Virginia
1637	Pequot War in New England
1640s	New England merchants enter slave trade Virginia forbids blacks to carry firearms
1650-1670	Judicial and legislative decisions in the Chesapeake region solidify racial lines
1651	Parliament passes first Navigation Act
1664	English conquer New Netherland
1673-1685	French expand into Mississippi valley

1675-1677	King Philip's War
1676	Bacon's Rebellion in Virginia
1682	La Salle sails down Mississippi River and claims Louisiana for France
1684	Massachusetts charter recalled
1686	Dominion of New England
1688	Glorious Revolution in England, followed by accession of William and Mary
1689	Overthrow of Governor Edmund Andros in New England Leisler's Rebellion in New York
1689-1697	King William's War
1690s	Transition from white indentured to black slave labor begins in Chesapeake
1692	Witchcraft crisis in Salem
1700	Spanish establish first mission in Arizona
1702-1713	Queen Anne's War
1713	Peace of Utrecht

Other Names to Know

Sir William Berkeley   Andrew Belcher
Metacomet   William Phips

(5) GLOSSARY OF IMPORTANT TERMS

black codes: laws borrowed from the English colonists in the Caribbean that severely limited black rights and activities

miscegenation: sexual union between members of different races

genocide: the willed extermination of a race or ethnic group by another

Glorious Revolution: the English revolution of 1688 that replaced James II with William and Mary. The revolution was based on the rejection of the "divine right" of kings and was a victory for Protestants, parliamentary power, and the English merchant and gentry class.

(6) ENRICHMENT IDEAS

1. After reviewing the questions in the Recovering the Past section about how tombstones reveal changing attitudes, especially toward religion, design some tombstones of your own, including both epitaph (inscription) and iconography (pictorial design). Make one or two for the mid-seventeenth century and one or two for the early eighteenth century. Finally, design a modern tombstone, perhaps for yourself or a friend, showing how epitaphs and iconography reflect contemporary attitudes and values.

2. Write a will for an individual colonist of the eighteenth century leaving items that were most likely to exist in an ordinary household.

3. Chart the main events in Anthony Johnson's life and the lives of his children. Then try to imagine how Anthony would explain each of the most important events. How might he explain the changing nature of race relations? What advice would you give to Johnson and his family?

4. In what ways does this chapter suggest that racism is a continuing part of American life? Which came first in American society, racism or slavery? What relevance does this chapter have for today? What social or international conflicts still occur between peoples?

(7) SAMPLE TEST AND EXAMINATION QUESTIONS

Multiple choice: Choose the best answer.

1. The fewest number of slaves in the seventeenth and eighteenth centuries were transported to
   a. the West Indies
   b. North America
   c. Spanish America
   d. Brazil

2. English colonists in the seventeenth century
   a. used black slaves as their main source of labor
   b. depended on Native Americans
   c. found the supply of white indentured servants sufficient for their needs
   d. needed no outside supply of workers

3. Slavery never became the foundation of the northern colonial work force because northerners
   a. had moral objections to it
   b. used hired hands to work their labor-intensive crops
   c. did not have any money to buy slaves
   d. had small family farms and did not need slaves

4. Compared to slaves in the rest of the New World, slaves in North America
   a. enjoyed a relatively healthy environment
   b. died off quickly because of disease
   c. had little opportunity to develop a culture because of their short life span
   d. had little opportunity for family life

5. All of the following statements are true about slavery EXCEPT
   a. a majority of southern slaves in the eighteenth century worked on plantations with at least ten other slaves
   b. slaves were widely dispersed among the northern population
   c. slaves were more frequently found in northern cities than in the countryside
   d. slaves were welcomed by white artisans who had more work than they could do themselves

6. Slave resistance in North America did not usually take the form of
   a. overt rebellion
   b. avoiding work
   c. running away
   d. arson and breaking tools

7. Black Christianity
   a. was drawn primarily from the religion of the master class
   b. blended African religious practices with those of the white church
   c. strongly influenced white religions
   d. rejected the whole idea of Protestant evangelicalism

8. A major barrier to slave family life was
   a. the imbalance of women to men
   b. white exploitation of black women
   c. polygamy
   d. too many single men

9. The underlying cause of King Philip's War was
   a. the trial and execution of three Wampanoags
   b. young tribesmen's anger over white encroachments on their lands
   c. King Philip's desire for an English wife
   d. all of the above

10. The results of King Philip's War included
    a. the extension of the New England frontier
    b. the rebuilding of all of New England's 90 towns
    c. the devastation of Indian society in New England
    d. the call for colonial unity

11. Bacon's Rebellion involved all of the following issues EXCEPT
    a. a lack of opportunity for land expansion
    b. declining tobacco prices and rising taxes, which aggravated social class conflict
    c. conflict between white frontiersmen and the Susquehannock Indians
    d. rivalry between free blacks and indentured servants for land near Williamsburg

12. Sir Edmund Andros outraged New Englanders by
    a. imposing taxes without legislative consent
    b. turning a Congregational church into an Anglican one
    c. establishing freedom of religion
    d. all of the above

13. The Salem witchcraft trials were evidence of
    a. the Devil's plan to destroy Puritanism
    b. an Indian plot to avenge white massacres
    c. the irrationality of teenage girls
    d. multiple tensions and hysteria growing from community instability

14. In the period of European rivalry in the late seventeenth and early eighteenth centuries, the colonies
    a. were not at all affected
    b. let the Iroquois do most of the fighting
    c. suffered grievously, especially in New England
    d. split evenly in support of the French and English

15. New France came into conflict with New England primarily because of
    a. religious and commercial rivalry
    b. competition for fertile farmlands
    c. the pressures of population
    d. none of the above

Identify and show a relationship between each of the following pairs:

James II	*and*	Governor Berkeley
Jacob Leisler	*and*	Sir Edmund Andros
Nathaniel Bacon	*and*	King Philip
La Salle	*and*	Peace of Utrecht

Essays

1. Explain why the late seventeenth century was a period of great instability and changing relationships in North America.

2. "The history of the colonies in the seventeenth century showed the impossibility of re-creating society on an English model. New conditions and unexpected new forces made it difficult to copy the familiar Old World in the New." Write an essay, using specific material from this chapter, to support this statement.

3. Black slaves faced the same problem of re-creating, or even preserving, cultural forms of their African past in North America. How successful were they in retaining what was familiar to them in the new conditions they found in the Americas? Support your answer with evidence drawn from this chapter.

4. Discuss four conflicts among different peoples and nations in the New World between 1675 and 1715.

Identify and Interpret: Chart

(that is, first, study the chart and describe what it shows; second, analyze the chart by explaining some of the reasons behind the patterns you see; third, assess the larger significance of the chart)

GROWTH OF THE COLONIAL POPULATION: WHITE AND BLACK				
Year	Estimated Total	White	Black	(Black as % of Total)
1640	26,634	26,037	596	(2%)
1670	111,935	107,400	4,535	(4%)
1700	250,888	223,071	27,817	(11%)
1740	905,563	755,539	150,024	(16.5%)
1770	2,148,076	1,688,254	459,822	(21%)

Source: U.S. Bureau of Census

4

The Maturing of Colonial Society

(1) CHAPTER OUTLINE

During a period of rapid growth, Devereaux Jarratt grows up in the family of a Virginia yeoman farmer. His interest in books and learning enables him to become a tutor for rich Virginia planter families. Eventually he rises to become an Anglican clergyman.

America's First Population Explosion
  The New Immigrants
  New Classes of Newcomers
  A Land of Opportunity?
  Africans in Chains

Beyond the Appalachians
  Cultural and Ecological Changes Among Interior Tribes
  France's Inland Empire
  Spain's America

A Land of Family Farms
  Northern Agricultural Society
  Changing Values
  Women in Northern Colonial Society

Ecological Transformation

The Plantation South
  The Tobacco Coast
  The Rice Coast
  The Backcountry
  Family Life in the South

The Urban World of Commerce and Ideas
  Sinews of Trade
  The Artisan's World
  Urban Social Structure
  The Entrepreneurial Ethos
  The American Enlightenment

The Great Awakening
Fading Faith
The Awakeners' Message
The Urban North
The Rural South
Legacy of the Awakening

Political Life
Structuring Colonial Governments
The Crowd in Action
The Growing Power of the Assemblies
Local Politics
The Spread of Whig Ideology

Conclusion: America in 1750

(2) SIGNIFICANT THEMES AND HIGHLIGHTS

1. In the first half of the eighteenth century, America was made up of several distinct regional societies, each in the process of growth and change. Beyond the Appalachians, extensive contact with France's growing inland empire and Spanish American settlements in the South and Southwest transformed Native American ways of life. English settlements, however, exploding in population, threatened Indian cultural cohesion the most. This chapter stresses the increasing complexity, adaption, and maturing of colonial English society. The eighteenth century provided opportunities for some, like Devereaux Jarratt; great gains for a few, like Boston merchant Andrew Belcher; but disappointment and privation for many others.

2. The farming society of the North was characterized by widespread land ownership and a rough kind of economic equality. In the South, plantation society was marked by the emergence of a gentry class and a labor force almost entirely made up of black slaves, while the backcountry, still in the frontier stages and settled by thousands of Scots-Irish and German immigrants, lacked the sharp class distinctions of the tidewater region. Colonial cities, with their highly differentiated class structure and new commercial values, were on the "cutting edge" of change. In each area, women played an important but limited role in daily life.

3. The Great Awakening was more than a religious revival, for it produced patterns of thought and behavior that helped to fuel the Revolution. The course of the Great Awakening in Boston and Virginia vividly shows the way in which its message fused with local social and economic tensions to threaten established authority.

4. Although many historians focus on the changing political arrangements in the colonies in the first half of the eighteenth century as a means of preparing for a discussion of the Revolution, this chapter makes the point that the fluidity of American society itself must be understood as a prelude to the events of the 1770s.

(3) LEARNING GOALS

Familiarity with Basic Knowledge

After reading this chapter, you should be able to:

1. Name the major immigrant groups coming to the colonies in the early eighteenth century, describe their social backgrounds, find their destinations on the map, and summarize their relative opportunities for social and economic advancement.

2. Describe the cultural changes of the interior Indian tribes as a result of their contact with French, Spanish, and English settlements in economic, social, and domestic life; in their relation to the environment; in political organization; and in intertribal tensions.

3. Describe northern farm society and its most important social characteristics and problems, including family life and the ways in which the roles and rights of women changed in the colonies.

4. Give an account of the "profound social transition" of the Upper South, characterize the social and political nature of the southern gentry, and detail the social and economic differences between the tobacco and rice coasts and the backcountry.

5. Describe the urban social structure, including the merchant's pivotal role, and the work pattern and attitudes of urban artisans.

6. Explain the major events and message of the Great Awakening, including its comparative impact on New England and the southern colonies and its effects on colonial political life.

Practice in Historical Thinking Skills

After reading this chapter, you should be able to:

1. Compare and contrast the development and maturing of English society in the farming northern colonies, in the plantation South, and in colonial cities.

2. Discuss the foundations of colonial political structures and ideology, including what colonists meant by a political balance of power and how it matched the reality of Whig ideology and local political arrangements.

3. Analyze how the changing mixture of ethnic, racial, religious, and regional settlements in North America, as well as class differences, provided awkward incongruities and threats of social unrest in the various societies of the New World.

(4) IMPORTANT DATES AND NAMES TO KNOW

1662	Half-Way Covenant in New England
1685	Beginning of 30-year stagnation in the tobacco market
1704	*Boston News-Letter,* first colonial newspaper, published
1713	Beginning of Scots-Irish and German immigration
1715-1730	Volume of slave trade doubles
1718	French settle New Orleans
1720s	Black population begins to increase naturally
1733	Benjamin Franklin publishes first *Poor Richard's Almanack*
1734-1736	Great Awakening begins in Northampton, Massachusetts
1735	Zenger acquitted of seditious libel in New York
1739-1740	Whitefield's first American tour spreads Great Awakening Slaves compose 90 percent of population on Carolina rice coast
1740s	Indigo becomes staple crop in Lower South
1747	Impressment riot in Boston
1760	Africans compose 20 percent of American population
1760s-1770s	Spanish establish California mission system
1769	American Philosophical Society founded at Philadelphia

Other Names to Know

Jonathan Edwards   Benjamin Franklin
Gilbert Tennent   James Davenport
César Ghiselin   Thomas Hancock
Francis Richardson

(5) GLOSSARY OF IMPORTANT TERMS

artisan: a skilled worker, using hand tools, usually in a small shop, such as a carpenter, cooper, shoemaker, or silversmith

Half-Way Covenant: an attempt by New England clergy in 1662 to counteract declining church membership by allowing the children of church members to join the church even though they had not experienced salvation; they were, however, denied voting and communion rights

franchise: the right to vote, widespread among colonial free white males

power of the purse: the power of colonial legislatures in the eighteenth century to initiate money bills, specifying the amount to be raised and its uses

(6) ENRICHMENT IDEAS

1. If you have been to a church recently, reflect on the sermon (lesson, homily) in terms of the Recovering the Past section for this chapter: What were the themes? Did they reflect current social or moral issues? Was the sermon a "jeremiad"? How might a future historian interpret it as a glimpse into the values of our time? If you have not been to church recently, try it as a would-be historian.

2. If you live in the East, you will probably be able to visit a historic house that dates from this period. In the South, see the country houses of the new gentry class or their town houses in Williamsburg. In the North and the Mid-Atlantic states, there are fine old houses of the merchant class and often of German immigrants. What do the houses suggest about daily life and about the class structure of the eighteenth century? Do you see evidences of slaves or servants? What suggestions are there about the lives of women and children? What would you conclude about the nature of work and leisure? Does the historic preservation of a house present a romanticized version of life in the past?

3. Consider recent episodes of religious revivalism. What has changed and what is the same?

4. Does the existence of pluralistic ethnic, racial, religious, and regional groups strengthen or threaten American cultural and political life today?

(7) SAMPLE TEST AND EXAMINATION QUESTIONS

Multiple choice: Choose the best answer.

1. Which of the following correctly arranges the immigrant groups in terms of size in the eighteenth century (largest first)?
    a. Africans, Scots-Irish, Germans, Swiss
    b. Germans, Africans, Scots-Irish, Swiss
    c. Scots-Irish, Germans, Swiss, Africans
    d. Africans, Germans, Scots-Irish, Swiss

2. The fastest-growing area in the early eighteenth century was
   a. New England
   b. South Carolina
   c. the northern frontier
   d. the area south of Pennsylvania

3. Most eighteenth-century emigrants were
   a. wealthy landed aristocrats
   b. middle-class artisans and yeoman farmers
   c. slaves and indentured servants
   d. prisoners

4. Most eighteenth-century indentured servants
   a. died or ran away before their time of service was over
   b. were brought from Africa
   c. usually were able to buy land after serving their time
   d. completed their time but rarely became independent property owners

5. Contact with the European colonists changed all of the following Indian cultural characteristics EXCEPT
   a. their matrilineal family life and clear division of work roles
   b. their local political organization
   c. their spiritual relation to the environment
   d. their system of law and justice and basic family organization

6. Northern farming society was characterized by
   a. a small class of rich, large farmers
   b. large numbers of poverty-stricken farmers
   c. widespread ownership of moderate-size farms
   d. a large renter class

7. Colonial American women in the eighteenth century
   a. rarely married for love
   b. could get divorced if their marriages failed
   c. had limited but significant responsibilities in their families and neighborhoods
   d. forfeited all property rights when they married

8. All of the following statements describe the Upper South tobacco coast in the eighteenth century EXCEPT
   a. slaves replaced indentured servants as the labor force
   b. agriculture became more diversified
   c. single white males still outnumbered white women
   d. a majority of families owned no slaves

9. In the backcountry of the South, settlers
   a. were German and Scots-Irish
   b. pursued mixed farming and cattle raising
   c. had few institutions
   d. all of the above

10. In the eighteenth century, what percentage of Americans lived in cities?
    a. 5 percent
    b. 10 percent
    c. 15 percent
    d. 20 percent

11. Urban artisans
    a. easily expected a rapid rise to ownership of their own shops
    b. took fierce pride in themselves as community leaders
    c. viewed themselves as "mere mechanics"
    d. read Ben Franklin's *Poor Richard's Almanack* regularly for advice

12. All of the following statements about eighteenth-century cities are true EXCEPT
    that they
    a. showed an increasing gap between rich and poor
    b. showed evidence of a new entrepreneurial ethic
    c. were marked by episodes of intensely violent social conflict
    d. devised new ways of dealing with the poor

13. In the early eighteenth century, most Americans
    a. were Congregationalists
    b. were Anglicans
    c. were Baptists
    d. belonged to no church at all

14. The Great Awakening
    a. decreased the number of religious sects
    b. undermined church-state ties
    c. led to the notion that community unity was attainable
    d. encouraged higher education by emphasizing that the clergy should be educated
       in the established church

15. American political assumptions included the belief that
    a. only free men with property should vote
    b. only men of wealth and social status should hold positions of political power
    c. people had the right to protest openly if power was abused
    d. all of the above

16. In the mid-eighteenth century, colonial assemblies
    a. gradually gained more powers, such as that of initiating money bills
    b. were mainly advisory bodies
    c. were regularly dissolved by royal governors
    d. ignored instructions from local constituencies

Essays

1. The three items under "Practice in Historical Thinking Skills" can serve as the basis for essays.

2. The Great Awakening transformed American life and thought in significant ways. Support this statement using appropriate evidence.

3. Rising tensions among social classes characterized colonial society in the eighteenth century and made political and religious struggles bitter. Discuss with evidence.

4. Explain the distribution of slave owners among white families in the South.

Identify and Interpret: Quotation
(that is, state who, what, where, when, and why significant)

The bow of God's wrath is bent, and the arrow made ready on the string; and justice bends the arrow at your heart, and strains the bow; and it is nothing but the mere pleasure of God, and that of an angry God, without any promise or obligation at all, that keeps the arrow one moment from being made drunk with your blood. Thus are all you that never passed under a great change of heart, by the mighty power of the Spirit of God upon your souls; all you that were never born again, and made new creatures. . . . The God that holds you over the pit of hell, much as one holds a spider or some loathsome insect over the fire, abhors you, and is dreadfully provoked; his wrath towards you burns like fire; he looks upon you as worthy of nothing else, but to be cast into the fire.

BENJAMIN FRANKLIN'S LIGHTNING ROD

In 1746, Benjamin Franklin, already a successful printer and civic organizer, began experimenting with electricity. That year, Dutchman Pieter van Musschenbroek had learned how to condense electricity in a glass bottle (called a Leyden jar) and to produce electrical sparks by attaching a conductor to the two sides of the bottle. Throughout Europe, amateur scientists began to play with this device, but nobody really understood the source or the nature of the mysterious electrical "fluid."

By 1748, Franklin had constructed a number of experiments in his house in Philadelphia for producing brilliant sparks from Leyden jars. His *Experiments and Observations on Electricity* was published in London in 1751, putting his name on the lips of scientists all over Europe. Far more important than Franklin's household experiments, however, was his development of the technical means to test what many already believed—that lightning produced by thunderstorms was a form of electricity. Franklin reasoned that a common kite could give him access to the electrical charges in clouds. He stretched a large silk handkerchief across two crossed sticks of wood, fitted the kite with a tail, and attached a "sharp-pointed wire" to the top. To the end of the twine by which he held the kite aloft, Franklin fastened a metal key, and to that a silk ribbon that he held in his hand. "As soon as any of the thunder-clouds come over the kite," Franklin wrote, "the pointed wire will draw the electric fire from them, and the kite, with all the twine, will be electrified. . . . And when the rain has wet the kite and twine, so that it can conduct the electric fire freely, you will find it stream out plentifully from the key on the approach to your knuckle." Franklin claimed that the similar appearance and behavior of lightning sparks and electrical ones proved that the "fluid" streaming from the key was the same as the electricity produced in Leyden jars. His experiment constituted a breakthrough of one of the most formidable barriers of the unknown and opened up an entirely new field of controlled study. After the kite experiment was publicized in Europe, Franklin's achievements catapulted him to the forefront of the world's scientists and earned him the Copley Medal of the Royal Society of London, one of the most advanced scientific bodies in the world.

Franklin personified the eighteenth-century Enlightenment in his desire to understand the laws that govern the natural world and in his determination to use these ideas, or what we would call scientific theory, to harness nature. In his experiments he encountered one of the most destructive natural forces, for electricity, in the form of lightning, destroyed buildings and ships with awful regularity. But once Franklin had learned the properties of electricity and had established that lightning was a form of it, it became relatively easy to contrive a metal rod, coated to prevent rusting, that would "throw off" the electricity and render it harmless. By 1753, convinced that he had mastered the theory of electricity and lightning, Franklin published a practical, essay, "How to Secure Houses &c. from Lightning," in his best-selling *Poor Richard's Almanack*. Here he explained a natural phenomenon that had always terrified people, and he provided the world with a relatively simple and inexpensive device to protect lives and property. Soon lightning rods shot up on houses and barns all over the American colonies. Farmers, homeowners, mariners, and church wardens could soon rest easier, knowing that their barns, houses, ships, and churches were safe. What had seemed to be the wrathful work of an angry God now became a force within the power of human beings to control. If the power of lightning could be harnessed by the son of a Boston candlemaker far from the centers of learning in Europe, what other forces of nature might be understood and brought under rein?

5

Bursting the Colonial Bonds

(1) CHAPTER OUTLINE

Shoemaker Ebenezer MacIntosh finds that the Stamp Act crisis offers him opportunities for influence and prominence. He leads mobs during the Stamp Act crisis protesting against both English authority and Boston's elite.

The Climactic Seven Years' War
    War and the Management of Empire
    Outbreak of Hostilities
    Tribal Strategies
    Consequences of War

The Crisis with England
    Sugar, Currency, and Stamps
    Stamp Act Riots
    An Uncertain Interlude
    The Growing Rift
    The Final Rupture

The Ideology of Revolutionary Republicanism
    A Plot Against Liberty
    Revitalizing American Society

The Turmoil of Revolutionary Society
    Urban People
    Women
    Protesting Farmers

Conclusion: Forging a Revolution

(2) SIGNIFICANT THEMES AND HIGHLIGHTS

1. Beginning with Ebenezer MacIntosh, the chapter stresses the role of common people in the events leading to the American Revolution rather than placing the usual emphasis on famous founding fathers.

2. The chapter shows that there was widespread group support for not one but two American revolutions. As MacIntosh's activities suggest, the "dual American Revolution" combined an external struggle to sever colonial ties to England with an internal struggle for control and reform of colonial society. The colonists sought liberation from English rule. But they also sought to combat the aristocratic, elitist nature of colonial society. The first revolution, marked by violent conflict with England, was the War for American Independence; the second, which involved intense class resentments, is called the American Revolution. The first ended in the Declaration of Independence; the second continued long into the next century.

3. The chapter not only explains these two revolutions but also interweaves colonial history with events in Europe and with the Native American tribes of the interior forests. The perspectives, survival strategies, and cultural changes of the Iroquois, Creek, and Cherokee are seen to be just as important as those of the British, French, and American colonists. The harmful effects of the Seven Years' War loom large in this chapter, especially on groups like the urban laboring poor, backcountry farmers, and women.

4. These groups each had their own struggles against concentrated wealth and power. But these differences were fruitful, for with educated lawyers and rich merchants and planters they fashioned a political ideology of revolutionary republicanism.

(3) LEARNING GOALS

Familiarity with Basic Knowledge

After reading this chapter, you should be able to:

1. Make a clear statement distinguishing between the War for American Independence and the American Revolution.

2. Describe the issues at stake in the series of wars of empire between England, Spain, France, and the several Native American Indian tribes, and outline the major developments and consequences of the Seven Years' War.

3. Outline the steps in the crisis with England between 1763 and 1776 leading to the War for American Independence.

4. Explain the essential issues and elements involved in the ideology of revolutionary republicanism.

5. Describe the grievances and concerns of ordinary Americans between 1763 and 1776, explaining how urban people, women, and farmers understood their "liberties" and "natural rights" in the early 1770s.

Practice in Historical Thinking Skills

After reading this chapter, you should be able to:

1. Discuss the two revolutions going on in the British colonies between 1763 and 1776, explaining the main characteristics of each and indicating which revolution you think motivated the American people more in the 1760s and 1770s.

2. Assess the mutual impact and influence of the interior Indian tribes, the American colonists, and the British and French on one another in the mid-eighteenth century.

3. Identify the chapter author's interpretation of "the nature of the American Revolution" and cite the evidence presented to support that point of view.

(4) IMPORTANT DATES AND NAMES TO KNOW

1696	Parliament established Board of Trade
1701	Iroquois establish policy of neutrality
1702-1713	Queen Anne's War
1713	Peace of Utrecht
1733	Molasses Act
1744-1748	King George's War
1754	Albany Congress convened
1755	Braddock defeated by French and Indian allies
1756-1763	Seven Years' War
1759	Wolfe defeats the French at Quebec
1759-1761	Cherokee War against the English
1760s	Economic slump in colonies
1763	Treaty of Paris ends Seven Years' War Proclamation line limits westward expansion
1764	Sugar and Currency acts Pontiac's Rebellion in Ohio valley

1765	Stamp Act
	Stamp Act Congress and resistance
1766	Declaratory Act
	Tenant rent war in New York
	Slave insurrections in South Carolina
1767	Townshend duties imposed
1768	British troops occupy Boston
1770	"Boston Massacre"
	Townshend duties repealed (except on tea)
1771	North Carolina Regulators defeated
1772	*Gaspee* incident in Rhode Island
1773	Tea Act provokes Boston Tea Party
1774	Parliament passes "Intolerable Acts"
	First Continental Congress meets (Philadelphia)
1775	Second Continental Congress meets (Philadelphia)
	Battles of Lexington and Concord (Massachusetts)
1776	Tom Paine publishes *Common Sense*
	Declaration of Independence

Other Names to Know

General James Wolfe	Pontiac
William Pitt	George Grenville
Patrick Henry	Lord North
John Adams	Samuel Adams
General Thomas Gage	Andrew Oliver
Governor Thomas Hutchinson	

(5) GLOSSARY OF IMPORTANT TERMS

privateers: privately outfitted ships licensed by colonial governments to attack French merchant shipping during the Seven Years' War

nonimportation and nonconsumption agreements: economic boycotts, as individual colonists pledged neither to import nor to use any British articles but rather to go without or to make their own, the main tactic of colonists protesting the Townshend duties and the Tea Act

revolutionary republicanism: a set of political ideals developed in the American Revolutionary era that emphasized anti-monarchy, liberty in balance with power, and political equality in tension with rule by an aristocracy of talent

(6) ENRICHMENT IDEAS

1. Study the Recovering the Past section for this chapter, noting how the inventories contribute to your understanding of the class tensions and internal social struggle that were part of the American Revolution.

2. If you live in a rural area or small town (especially in the Midwest), it is likely that your local newspaper will advertise several auctions of the property and household belongings of family farms in the process of dissolution. Go to an auction or two, and note how the items for sale reflect social class.

3. If you live in the East, you can visit such Revolutionary sites as Philadelphia, Boston, and Lexington and Concord, as well as battle sites at Bunker Hill (Breed's Hill), Saratoga, Trenton, Valley Forge, Brandywine, and Yorktown. What interpretation is provided at these sites? Which "American Revolution" is presented? Is there any indication of the social tensions of the inner war? How do you explain the approach taken at these Revolutionary-era sites?

(7) SAMPLE TEST AND EXAMINATION QUESTIONS

Multiple choice: Choose the best answer.

1. In seeking to survive the wars of empire in North America, the Native American Indian tribes
   a. depended on French friendship
   b. formed treaty alliances with the more numerous British
   c. pursued aggressive neutrality in which they shifted their allegiance between the British and the French
   d. formed intertribal confederacies

2. Most at stake for the European powers in the wars of empire was
   a. the economic and political value of North American land and resources
   b. religious freedom
   c. national pride
   d. treaty obligations to the Indians

3. The Seven Years' War
   a. spurred colonial prosperity
   b. required heavy taxes
   c. rendered the colonies vulnerable to fluctuations in the British economy
   d. all of the above

4. The British finally turned the tide of battle to their side in the Seven Years' War when they
   a. pursued William Pitt's policies in North America
   b. defeated the Iroquois allies of the French
   c. convinced the American colonists to share more of the fighting burdens of the war
   d. dispatched General Braddock to attack French forts

5. After the Treaty of Paris, economic prosperity in the colonies
   a. surged because of captured French resources
   b. turned to depression, especially among the laboring classes in coastal towns
   c. remained high because of war profiteering
   d. was largely unchanged

6. The Stamp Act riots
   a. hardened the British attitude toward the colonies
   b. revealed how united all American classes were in opposing British authority
   c. politicized the American people against both English rule and internal elites
   d. convinced Parliament to limit its authority over the colonies

7. The Sugar Act
   a. doubled duties on sugar imported from the West Indies
   b. kept duties the same but improved enforcement
   c. cut duties in half but improved enforcement
   d. required stamps on every gallon of imported molasses

8. In the early 1770s, a British proposal that deeply threatened and angered the colonists was one
   a. to tax window glass
   b. to have the British government rather than colonial assemblies pay the salaries of royal governors
   c. to limit town meetings to once a month
   d. to close the port of Boston permanently

9. Which is in the correct chronological order?
   a. Tea Act, Tea Party, Continental Congress, Intolerable Acts
   b. Tea Act, Intolerable Acts, Tea Party, Continental Congress
   c. Tea Act, Tea Party, Intolerable Acts, Continental Congress
   d. Intolerable Acts, Continental Congress, Tea Act, Tea Party

10. In the face of tougher expressions of British authority, by the end of 1774 the colonists had
    a. knuckled under to British rule
    b. created armed militia units to harass British troops and bully local Loyalist merchants
    c. sought aid from the French
    d. begun electing their own provincial assemblies to draft declarations of independence

11. The ideology of revolutionary republicanism included all of the following EXCEPT
    a. the rejection of monarchy
    b. concern over the dangers of governmental power
    c. a balance between liberty and power
    d. pure levelling political equality

12. Revolutionary agitation for equality and rights among social groups was expressed by all of the following EXCEPT
    a. urban artisans
    b. backcountry farmers
    c. Virginia planters
    d. women

13. The dual American Revolution
    a. united all colonial classes in a common effort
    b. exposed class tensions in the process of struggling against British tyranny
    c. tore the colonies apart
    d. put the colonists at war with both the French and British

14. The Declaration of Independence
    a. was a novel departure from the ideas in patriotic pamphlets and congressional addresses
    b. was the original brainchild of Thomas Jefferson
    c. was hotly debated by the Continental Congress
    d. was filled with familiar ideas from the colonists' British heritage

15. Energy for the American Revolution came from all of the following EXCEPT
    a. Anglican ministers from New York
    b. some wealthy Virginia planters and New England merchants
    c. urban artisans in Boston
    d. small farmers in western North Carolina

16. His pamphlet, *Common Sense*, encouraged America's revolt:
    a. Samuel Adams
    b. John Hancock
    c. Thomas Paine
    d. Patrick Henry

Identify and show a relationship between each of the following pairs:

Pontiac	*and*	Proclamation Line of 1763
"Liberty Tree"	*and*	Andrew Oliver
Thomas Hutchinson	*and*	Samuel Adams
William Pitt	*and*	Fort Duquesne
James Wolfe	*and*	Thomas Gage
George Grenville	*and*	Patrick Henry
John Hancock	*and*	Ebenezer MacIntosh
Sons of Liberty	*and*	Philadelphia militia
Stamp Act	*and*	Townshend Acts

Essays

1. Items 1-3 under "Practice in Historical Thinking Skills" in the "Learning Goals" section can be used as practice essay questions.

2. To ignore the role of Native Americans in the pre-Revolutionary era is to ignore a very real factor in the coming struggle. Discuss with suitable evidence.

3. Even with better will and more compromises on both sides, it would have been difficult to prevent the American War for Independence. It was, in short, inevitable. The "American Revolution," however, was not. Discuss.

4. It has been said that "the American Revolution was not made but prevented." Discuss what you think this means and the extent to which you agree.

Map Question:

Locate the following on the accompanying map.

1. Lake Champlain
2. Iroquois Confederacy
3. Cherokee nation
4. Ohio River valley
5. Fort Duquesne
6. New York City
7. Philadelphia
8. Charleston, South Carolina
9. Fort Ticonderoga
10. Creek nation
11. Jamestown
12. Fort Niagara
13. Boston
14. Quebec City

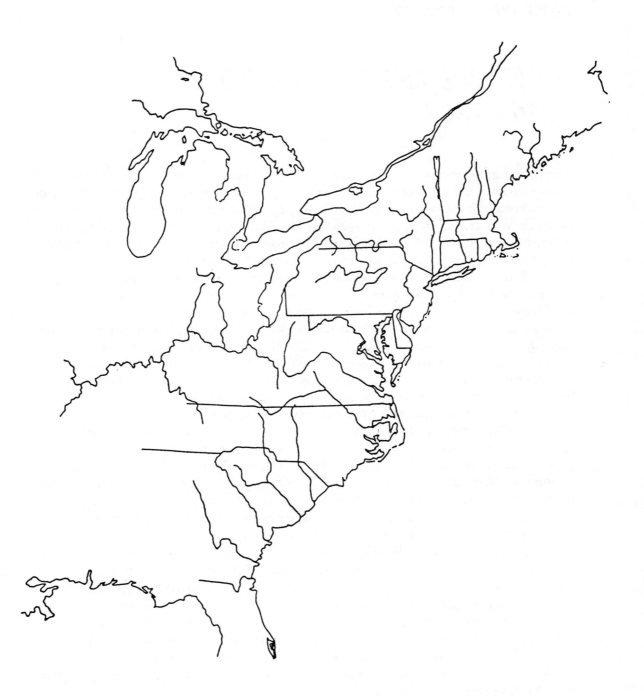

A REVOLUTIONARY PEOPLE
1776 - 1828

The American Revolution not only marked an epic military victory over the powerful mother country but also set the course of national development in ways that still affect American society. Members of the Revolutionary generation were inspired by the idea that once they were free from England, they would build a model society based on principles of freedom and equality. Even as the battle for independence raged, they embarked on the task of building new forms of government and transforming their social, religious, and economic lives. This attempt to construct a *novus ordo seclorum*, a new order of the ages, continued beyond the Revolutionary era and continues yet today.

Chapter 6, "A People in Revolution," traces the impact of the Revolutionary call to arms on the various groups—male and female, white, black, and Native American—that made up American society and traces the exhilarating yet divisive efforts to fashion a new, republican political order. Chapter 7, "Consolidating the Revolution," examines the critical years of the 1780s, when the new nation struggled to forge national unity following the Revolutionary War and to find security in a hostile Atlantic world. Out of that struggle and the continuing competition for political power in the states emerged a great debate over the country's governmental structure. That debate led to the replacement of the Articles of Confederation with a new constitution, which in turn helped to create a stronger government. Learning to live under the new constitution during the 1790s is the focus for Chapter 8, "Creating a Nation." During those tumultuous years, charged with the reverberations of the French Revolution and fierce disagreements about the government's role in economic affairs, Federalists and Jeffersonians battled for control of the new government and the chance to shape the nation's future.

Chapter 9, "Society and Politics in the Early Republic," delves into the political and diplomatic developments of the first three decades of the nineteenth century, when the young nation expanded rapidly beyond the Appalachians, acquired vast new territories, fought a series of wars with Indian nations and a second war against England, and moved toward a new party system, all under the presidencies of three Virginia Democratic-Republicans—Jefferson, Madison, and Monroe—and one New Englander, John Quincy Adams. Chapter 9 also investigates efforts by the American people in the areas of education, women's rights, and slavery to perfect their republican society in keeping with the lofty principles of the Revolution.

6

A People in Revolution

(2) SIGNIFICANT THEMES AND HIGHLIGHTS

1. As Long Bill Scott's sad but heroic story reveals, people in America during the Revolution struggled not only to create a nation but even more to improve their own lives. This chapter emphasizes the private struggles and hardships and the disrupted lives of people in America during the Revolutionary War rather than the battles and public policy decisions of the war. The chapter continues the account of class divisions in American society during wartime, which underlines the theme of a "dual revolution."

2. This chapter creates a mood that underlines the startling facts that the American Revolutionary War was the longest war in American history (except one), the most costly in per capita casualties (except one), and (without exception) the most damaging in terms of per capita victimization of civilians and the disruption and disarray of economic life.

3. It was in state politics that Americans transformed and expressed the political meaning of the Revolution. The making of new state governments involved converting the ideology of revolutionary republicanism into action, first by writing state constitutions and second by resolving the thorny issues of Revolutionary times.

4. Although many more ordinary people—white farmers, small shopkeepers, urban artisans, and the like—were politicized and joined the political process, there were limits to republican representation and political participation. Large numbers of Americans—women, blacks, Indians—were excluded from the new political system. This chapter captures their voices as they express their frustrations with a revolution that stopped short of the full realization of its ideological rhetoric.

(3) LEARNING GOALS

Familiarity with Basic Knowledge

After reading this chapter, you should be able to:

1. Describe the major British and American strategies in the American Revolution and state how well they worked.

2. Explain five reasons why the Americans defeated the British and won the war.

3. Describe the economic costs of the war to commerce, agriculture, and manufacturing.

4. Explain how the war affected slaves, Loyalists, and Native American Indians, especially the Iroquois.

5. List the questions that the early republican politicians (or anyone, for that matter) asked when thinking about creating new governments.

6. State a few key differences between the Pennsylvania and Massachusetts state constitutions.

7. State the ways in which Americans were politicized in the Revolutionary era.

Practice in Historical Thinking Skills

After reading this chapter, you should be able to:

1. Analyze how the American people made the shift from separating from an imperial system to the creation of a republican form of government.

2. Assess the extent to which the American Revolution, on balance, was good or bad for slaves, northern farmers, Loyalists, Native Americans, wealthy Patriots, and ordinary citizens.

3. Assess how well Americans were able to fulfill their revolutionary republican ideology in the war and the postwar era.

(4) IMPORTANT DATES AND NAMES TO KNOW

1775	Continental Congress urges "states" to establish new governments
	Lord Dunmore's proclamation to slaves and servants in Virginia
	Congress resolves on Indian friendship
	Iroquois Six Nations pledge neutrality
1776	Declaration of Independence
	British evacuate Boston and seize New York City
	States pass laws against Loyalists
	Eight states draft constitutions
	Cherokee raids and American retaliations
1777	British occupy Philadelphia
	Iroquois join the British (except Tuscarora and Oneida)
	British surrender at Saratoga
	Washington's army winters at Valley Forge
1778	War shifts to the South
	Savannah falls to the British
	French treaty of alliance and commerce
1779	Sullivan destroys Iroquois villages in New York
	Massachusetts state constitutional convention

1780	Charleston surrenders to the British
	Nathanael Greene begins partisan warfare in the South
	Pennsylvania begins gradual abolition of slavery
	Massachusetts constitution ratified

| 1780s | Virginia and Maryland debate abolition of slavery |
| | Destruction of Iroquois Confederacy |

| 1781 | Cornwallis surrenders at Yorktown (Virginia) |
| | Articles of Confederation ratified by states |

1783	Treaty of Paris (America and England sign peace)
	Massachusetts Supreme Court abolishes slavery
	King's Commission on American Loyalists

| 1790 | Slave trade outlawed in all states but two |

Other Names to Know

General William Howe
Silas Deane
Thomas Danforth
John Adams

Comte de Vergennes
Robert Morris
John Dickinson
Thomas Peters

(5) GLOSSARY OF IMPORTANT TERMS

partisan warfare: American strategy (called guerrilla warfare today) under Nathanael Greene in the South whereby several small, highly mobile bands of soldiers waged hit-and-run attacks on British troops rather than standing together as one army

privateering: government chartering of private vessels to prey upon English merchant ships

bills of credit: paper money issued by the continental government and backed by government credit to finance the war

Loyalists: Americans loyal to the crown during the Revolution who actively supported, sympathized with, or fought on the British side

sovereignty: source or locus of ultimate power. For republican ideology, sovereignty resided in the people.

(6) ENRICHMENT IDEAS

1. Explore in the Recovering the Past section the way in which enlistment and muster rolls reveal the social character of Revolutionary War soldiers. Do you think the poor shouldered an unnecessarily heavy burden of the fighting? Interview some veterans of recent American wars, or find studies of the social class and racial composition of modern soldiers. What do you conclude?

2. If you live in the East, visit Revolutionary War battle sites at Boston, New York, Trenton, Princeton, Bennington, Saratoga, Brandywine, Savannah, Charleston, Cowpens, Guilford Court House, or Yorktown. Imagine yourself a common soldier at one of those battles. Write a letter home or a diary entry describing what it was like.

3. Imagine you are a former crown official—or a slave—or a New England farmer—or a northern artisan—or a Virginia Patriot slave owner—or a woman living on the frontier—or some other colonist. What reasons would you give to explain your position for or against the war?

4. Difficult material like political ideology is sometimes easier to understand by representing abstract ideas in some sort of visual way. Construct a chart on revolutionary republican ideology, showing such things as political focus and structures (branches and levels of government), ways of balancing liberty and power, and ideas about equality and who should rule; for example, a continuum:

LIBERTY   POWER/ORDER

HAPPINESS   PROPERTY

the P E O P L E

or a diagram showing John Adams's "Thoughts on Government" and his proposal for the Massachusetts state constitution:

LEGISLATIVE		*EXECUTIVE*	*JUDICIARY*
REPRESENTATIVE ASSEMBLY	*SENATE* (Council)	*GOVERNOR* (President)	
•democratic	•aristocratic	•independent	•separate
•the many	•the few	•the one	and distinct
•liberty	•property	•balancer	

(7) SAMPLE TEST AND EXAMINATION QUESTIONS

Multiple choice: Choose the best answer.

1. The primary strategy of the American continental forces against the British was
   a. defensive, surviving by avoiding major battles
   b. aggressive, seeking to split British forces in half
   c. to hide while waiting for French help
   d. to let the British have coastal cities while protecting the frontier against Indians

2. All of the following were included in the Treaty of Paris (1783) EXCEPT
   a. the western boundary of the United States was set at the Mississippi River
   b. all debts between citizens of the two countries were invalidated
   c. the British recognized the independence of the United States of America
   d. the Americans promised to restore Loyalists' rights and properties

3. The Americans were successful at the Paris treaty convention because
   a. they had the support of the French foreign minister, Vergennes
   b. they ignored the French and negotiated directly with the British
   c. they held Cornwallis hostage until they received generous terms
   d. Franklin and Adams respected instructions from Congress

4. The continental army was made up largely of
   a. poor men conscripted or hired as substitutes by wealthy men in towns filling their quotas
   b. patriotic gentlemen and yeoman farmers
   c. a polyglot mixture of local militias
   d. eager volunteer enlisted men

5. Economic costs of the Revolutionary War included all of the following EXCEPT
   a. rampant inflation
   b. the collapse of the monetary system
   c. the destruction of home manufacturing
   d. the disruption of commerce

6. The American Patriots won the war against Great Britain for all of following reasons EXCEPT
   a. the administrative talents and determination of General Washington
   b. British caution and lack of will
   c. the enormous drain on England's financial resources
   d. the military skill of the state militias

7. Which one did Congress *not* use to pay for the war:
   a. issuing bills of credit
   b. printing money
   c. levying income taxes
   d. loans from the French and the Dutch

8. Economically, the Revolution
   a. damaged the New England fishing industry
   b. caused trade shifts that opened highly profitable new non-English markets
   c. helped agriculture because the army needed supplies
   d. hurt manufacturing

9. The Iroquois resolve to remain neutral during the Revolution
   a. reflected a new strategy of surviving conflicts among whites in the New World
   b. was abandoned at the Oswego Council when most of the Iroquois nations joined the British against the Americans
   c. resulted in generous land concessions under the Treaty of Paris
   d. was abandoned to side with the French in exchange for trade goods, arms, and protection

10. The Revolutionary generation agreed that basic to the idea of constitutionalism were all of the following EXCEPT
    a. constitutions should be written
    b. governments should exist first in order to prepare constitutions
    c. the constitutions were produced by the people
    d. elected rather than appointed representatives were crucial in writing constitutions

11. The Pennsylvania constitution provided for
    a. an executive governor without veto power
    b. two representative legislatures
    c. an executive created out of the assembly
    d. no governor

12. The Massachusetts constitution was based on John Adams's ideas of
    a. the predominance of aristocratic power
    b. a weak executive branch
    c. mixed and balanced separate branches of government
    d. power in the lower house

13. The American people were politicized during the American Revolution by
    a. ministers
    b. an outpouring of political pamphlets and newspapers
    c. the frequency of state-level elections
    d. all of the above

14. For the colonial soldiers in the Revolution, which proved most deadly:
    a. Indian attacks
    b. British bullets
    c. diseases and sickness
    d. French cannons

Date and put the following events in the correct chronological order:

Lexington and Concord   Boston Tea Party
Treaty of Paris   Stamp Act
Constitutional Convention   Battle of Saratoga
end of Seven Years' War   Declaration of Independence
Yorktown   Treaty of Fort Stanwix

Identify and show a relationship between each of the following pairs:

Treaty of Fort Stanwix   *and*   Treaty of Hopewell
Silas Deane   *and*   Robert Morris
partisan warfare   *and*   Valley Forge
Saratoga   *and*   French treaty of alliance and commerce
Elizabeth Drinker   *and*   Cherry Valley, New York

Essays

1. Assess the extent to which the American Revolution, on balance, was good or bad for *five* of the following groups: northern farmers, Virginia slave owners, slaves, Native Americans, Loyalists, urban artisans and shopkeepers, frontier women.

2. Assess how well Americans were able to fulfill their revolutionary republican ideology in the war and the postwar era.

3. Show how the ideology of republicanism, which developed during the war, reflected the colonial experience with England prior to the war.

Identify and Interpret: Quotation
(that is, state who, what, where, when, and why significant)

I cannot say that I think you are very generous to the ladies; for, whilst you are proclaiming peace and goodwill to men, emancipating all nations, you insist upon retaining an absolute power over wives. But you must remember, that arbitrary power is like most other things which are very hard, very liable to be broken; and, notwithstanding all your wise laws and maxims, we have it in our power, not only to free ourselves, but to subdue our masters, and, without violence, throw both your natural and legal authority at our feet.

7

Consolidating the Revolution

(1) CHAPTER OUTLINE

Timothy Bloodworth of New Hanover County, North Carolina, rises from humble origins and gains a substantial position in his community and the respect of his neighbors. Although he becomes a delegate to the Confederation Congress in 1784, he soon loses confidence in the Articles of Confederation and supports the call for a special convention to meet in Philadelphia in 1787. When he views the constitution that emerges from that convention, however, he fears that the gains of the Revolution will be lost. He works tirelessly to defeat the new proposal. As a result of his efforts and the efforts of men like him, North Carolina only endorsed the new union when the Congress had forwarded a national bill of rights to the state for its approval.

Struggling with the Peacetime Agenda
    Demobilizing the Army
    Opening the West
    Wrestling with the National Debt
    Surviving in a Hostile World

Political Tumult in the States
    The Limits of Republican Experimentation
    Shays's Rebellion

Toward A New National Government
    The Rise of Federalism
    The Grand Convention
    Federalists Versus Anti-Federalists
    The Struggle over Ratification
    The Social Geography of Ratification

Conclusion: Completing the Revolution

(2) SIGNIFICANT THEMES AND HIGHLIGHTS

1. As the anecdote of Timothy Bloodworth suggests, this chapter explores the uncertain world facing Americans after the Revolutionary War had ended. Many feared the new

government would not be able to assure settlement of the country's interior or pay off the massive war debt. The new nation was a weak newcomer in a world still dominated by powers like Great Britain.

2. The frantic pace of political experimentation on the state level moderated after 1783 as conservative arrangements replaced some of the radical ones passed only a few years earlier. As Shays's Rebellion suggested, however, many had not forgotten the cries for equal rights and popular consent that had been so powerfully expressed in 1776.

3. This chapter presents the political controversies marking the writing and ratification of the Constitution and explains the struggle for ratification of that document.

(3) LEARNING GOALS

Familiarity with Basic Knowledge

After reading this chapter, you should be able to:

1. Describe the terms of the land ordinances of 1785 and 1787 and the ideas behind the conquest theory.

2. Itemize the steps taken by Robert Morris to deal with the national debt.

3. Explain the causes and consequences of Shays's Rebellion.

4. Describe the reasons for dissatisfaction with the Articles of Confederation.

5. State the major compromises worked out at the Constitutional Convention and the major features of the original Constitution—its organizational format and the most significant allocations of power, rights, and responsibilities.

6. Outline the major arguments of Federalists and Anti-Federalists in the debates over ratification of the Constitution.

Practice in Historical Thinking Skills

After reading this chapter, you should be able to:

1. Explain the reasons for the success of the Federalists in writing and securing the ratification of the Constitution.

2. Analyze how the Constitution changed and strengthened the government that had existed under the Articles of Confederation.

3. Describe the different political and social perspectives of the Federalists and Anti-Federalists.

(4) IMPORTANT DATES AND NAMES TO KNOW

1784	Treaty of Fort Stanwix with the Iroquois Spain closes Mississippi River to American navigation
1784-1786	Agrarian protest in several states
1785	Treaty of Hopewell with the Cherokee Land Ordinance for Northwest Territory Jay-Gardoqui negotiations
1786	Annapolis convention calls for revision of Articles of Confederation Virginia adopts "Bill for Establishing Religious Freedom"
1786-1787	Shays's Rebellion (Massachusetts)
1787	Northwest Ordinance Constitutional Convention convened (Philadelphia) *Federalist Papers* published by Hamilton, Jay, and Madison
1788	Constitution ratified

Other Names to Know

James Madison	Alexander Hamilton
John Jay	Robert Morris

(5) GLOSSARY OF IMPORTANT TERMS

ordinance: a governmental law or regulation

relief ("stay") laws: state laws desired by debtors and farmers in hard times that would suspend the collection of private debts and the foreclosure of farms for a specified period

ratification: formal sanctioning of a document such as a proposed constitution or treaty

federalism: a system where political power is divided between a central (national) government and smaller governmental units called states or provinces

(6) ENRICHMENT IDEAS

1. Find an Indian treaty for the Native Americans in your region and discover what it suggests about the attitudes and values of both the white and Native American treaty-makers.

2. The complete text of the United States Constitution is found in the Appendix of *The American People*. Read and study the Constitution, breaking it down into its major parts, and identify the five or so most significant points to remember in each part.

3. Make a chart contrasting the major differences between the Declaration of Independence and the Constitution over their primary purposes, the quality and style of language, political ideology, assumptions about human nature and ends of government, and how to achieve political change.

(7) SAMPLE TEST AND EXAMINATION QUESTIONS

Multiple choice: Choose the best answer.

1. After the Revolution, the Confederation Congress
   a. successfully opened western lands
   b. quelled Indian resistance to white western migration
   c. was unable to open the interior
   d. gave all western lands to speculators

2. Shays's Rebellion revealed that
   a. farmers wanted more gold coins in circulation
   b. authority under the Articles of Confederation was too weak
   c. the American Revolution had succeeded in shifting the balance of power from the rich to the poor
   d. the court system was responsive to the needs of the people

3. The Federalists believed all of the following EXCEPT that
   a. the national government should be stronger
   b. there were "natural distinctions" between people
   c. there was a crisis threatening the nation's survival
   d. the states should assume more powers

4. After the Revolution, the Confederation Congress treated Native Americans of the interior
   a. as if they were sovereign nations
   b. as if they were military foes
   c. no differently than they had in colonial times
   d. as if they were conquered peoples

5. The Virginia Plan differed most significantly from the New Jersey Plan by calling for
   a. a bicameral Congress and a whole new national government
   b. revision of the Articles of Confederation by letting Congress choose a president
   c. revision of the Articles by providing for equal representation in both houses of Congress
   d. the abolition of the executive branch

6. The Constitution clearly shows that the founding fathers
   a. wanted to abolish slavery
   b. were prepared to lay the groundwork for eventual equal rights between whites and blacks
   c. provided for the protection of slavery
   d. were willing to abolish only three-fifths of the slaves

7. That the Constitution shifted power from the states to the central government is made evident by giving Congress power
   a. to lay and collect taxes
   b. to regulate foreign and domestic commerce
   c. to pass all laws "necessary and proper" for carrying out other powers
   d. all of the above

8. According to the Constitution, Congress has all of the following powers EXCEPT the power
   a. to declare war
   b. to borrow money
   c. to tax exports
   d. to lay and collect taxes

9. According to the Constitution, the executive branch has all of the following powers EXCEPT that of
   a. declaring wars
   b. enforcing laws
   c. making judicial appointments
   d. commanding the army and navy

10. According to the Constitution, treaties, in order to become the law of the land, must be approved by
    a. a majority of the Supreme Court
    b. two-thirds of the House
    c. two-thirds of the Senate
    d. three-fourths of both houses of Congress

11. Anti-Federalists believed that
    a. the Constitutional Convention was unfortunate but thoroughly legal
    b. separation of powers was enough to prevent the abuse of power in the new government
    c. republican liberty was best preserved by the balancing of factions
    d. republican liberty was best preserved in small, simple, homogeneous societies

12. Madison argued in *Federalist No. 10* that factions were
    a. less likely to destroy liberty in a large republic than in a small one
    b. more likely to destroy liberty in a large republic than in a small one
    c. undemocratic and therefore should be suppressed
    d. good for homogeneous states but unnecessary in a federal system

13. The ratification process revealed that Federalist strength was strongest
    a. in small interior farm regions
    b. in coastal cities and towns
    c. in the South except for Georgia
    d. among merchants but not working-class artisans and workers

True or False: Questions on the U.S. Constitution

___1. The Constitution (plus laws and treaties) is the supreme law of the land.

___2. The Constitution created a Supreme Court and 13 district courts.

___3. Congress has the power to coin money.

___4. Congress may not tax exports.

___5. The president makes treaties with the approval of two-thirds of Congress.

___6. The president appoints ambassadors, judges, and other officials with the advice and consent of the Senate.

___7. To be a senator, one must be at least 35 years old.

___8. Treason consists of levying war against the United States or giving aid and comfort to the enemy.

___9. Slaves and indentured servants count as three-fifths of a person for purposes of representation.

___10. All bills for raising revenue must originate in the House of Representatives.

___11. New states may be admitted to the Union by Congress.

___12. The United States may intervene against domestic violence within a state.

___13. The president declares war with the approval of two-thirds of Congress.

___14. The phrase "life, liberty, and the pursuit of happiness" from the Declaration of Independence reappears in the Constitution.

___15. The president shares with federal courts the power "to faithfully execute the laws."

___16. Amendments may be proposed by either two-thirds of Congress or the states (in legislatures or conventions) and must be ratified by three-quarters of the states (in legislatures or conventions).

___17. The First Amendment guarantees the rights of speech, press, petition, religion, and bearing of arms.

___18. The president may veto decisions of the Supreme Court.

Essays

1. Explain why the Articles of Confederation were considered too weak for the fledgling republic.

2. Show how the roots of the main provisions of the Constitution are in the colonial experience under English rule as well as in the Articles of Confederation period.

3. To what extent do you agree with Fisher Ames's question as to whether the rulers in a democracy may use physical force to maintain domestic order without turning public opinion against them? Discuss, drawing your evidence from the history of the United States in the 1780s.

Identify and Interpret: Quotation
(that is, state who, what, where, when, and why significant)

*That this is a consolidated government is demonstrably clear; and the danger of such a government is, to my mind, very striking. I have the highest veneration for those gentlemen; but, sir, say, **We, the people**? My political curiosity, exclusive of my anxious solicitude for the public welfare, leads me to ask, Who authorized them to speak the language of **We the people**, instead of, **We, the states**? States are the characteristics and the soul of a confederation.*

8

Creating a Nation

(1) CHAPTER OUTLINE

David Brown, Revolutionary War veteran, seaman, and pamphleteer, increasingly attacked the central government under the new national constitution in the 1790s. He claimed it was a conspiracy of the rich to exploit farmers, artisans, and other common folk. His inflammatory charges aroused the ire of the federal judiciary, which convicted him of sedition and put him in prison. He was released only after the election of Thomas Jefferson in 1800.

Launching the National Republic
> Beginning the New Government
> The Bill of Rights
> The People Divide
> The Whiskey Rebellion

The Republic in a Threatening World
> The Promise and Peril of the French Revolution
> Citizen Genêt and the Democratic-Republican Societies
> Jay's Controversial Treaty

Federalists Versus Jeffersonians
> The Election of 1796
> The War Crisis with France
> The Alien and Sedition Acts
> Local Reverberations
> The "Revolution of 1800"

Conclusion: Toward the Nineteenth Century

(2) SIGNIFICANT THEMES AND HIGHLIGHTS

1. As David Brown's story suggests, this chapter presents the turbulent political controversies surrounding the launching of the new government in the 1790s.

2. The struggle to create a nation was marked by the formation of two political parties, Federalists and Democratic-Republicans, and by crises in the young nation's

relationships with France and England during the presidential administrations of George Washington and John Adams.

3. Underlying the political controversies of the 1790s, as David Brown's life reveals, were class differences between rich and poor, regional differences between the urban Northeast and the interior West and South, and two conflicting ideological views over issues of power, political equality, and the proper role of central government in a republican society.

(3) LEARNING GOALS

Familiarity with Basic Knowledge

After reading this chapter, you should be able to:

1. Describe the Bill of Rights and its significance.

2. Outline Hamilton's view of the proper role of government, his financial plan, and the fate of each proposal.

3. Explain the major events of George Washington's administration, including the causes of the Whiskey Rebellion.

4. State how the French Revolution divided Americans and contributed to the development of party politics.

5. Describe the social composition, political principles, and activities of the Democratic-Republican societies.

6. Describe the major domestic and foreign crises of the administration of John Adams.

Practice in Historical Thinking Skills

After reading this chapter, you should be able to:

1. Discuss the disagreement over the role of government in the new nation.

2. Compare and contrast the differing ideological positions and visions of the Federalists and the Democratic-Republicans in the 1790s.

3. Decide whether the election of 1800 was, as Jefferson thought, "a revolution in the principles of our government."

(4) IMPORTANT DATES AND NAMES TO KNOW

1789	Inauguration of Washington as first president Outbreak of French Revolution
1790	Hamilton's "Reports on the Public Credit" Slave trade outlawed in all states except Georgia and South Carolina
1791	Bill of Rights ratified Whiskey tax established Bank of the United States chartered Hamilton's "Report on Manufactures"
1793	Controversy over Citizen Genêt's visit
1793-1794	Outbreak of war in Europe Whiskey Rebellion in Pennsylvania
1795	Jay's Treaty with England divides nation
1796	Washington's Farewell Address John Adams elected president
1797	XYZ affair in France
1798	Naturalization Act; Alien and Sedition Acts Virginia and Kentucky resolutions
1798-1800	Undeclared naval war with France
1799	Trials of David Brown and Luther Baldwin
1800	Adams achieves "peace" with France
1801	Jefferson elected president by House of Representatives

Other Names to Know

James Madison	John Jay
Aaron Burr	Talleyrand
John Marshall	

(5) GLOSSARY OF IMPORTANT TERMS

federalism: a system where political power is divided between a central (national) government and smaller governmental units called states or provinces

70

federalists: supporters of the ratification of the Constitution and the shift of power from local and state governments to the central government

Federalists: political party organized in the 1790s under Alexander Hamilton and John Adams dedicated to a strong central government, national power and economic growth, and rule by the wealthy elite

Democratic-Republican societies: popular associations in America that supported the ideals of revolutionary France and became the basis of the Jeffersonian Republican party

(6) ENRICHMENT IDEAS

1. After examining the paintings in the Recovering the Past section and opening for this chapter, look up and study patriotic paintings of the Revolutionary era by John Barralet, John Trumbull, Gilbert Stuart, Charles Willson Peale, and others. What kind of mythology do they depict about the founding fathers? What kinds of mythologies exist today about American heroes? Are our heroes still political figures? If not, who are they? What does the choice of a nation's heroes suggest about that nation's values?

2. Make a chart contrasting the major ideas, political principles, and social composition of the two emerging political party traditions.

(7) SAMPLE TEST AND EXAMINATION QUESTIONS

Multiple choice: Choose the best answer.

1. The Bill of Rights was
   a. part of the original Constitution
   b. a leftover from the Articles of Confederation
   c. a means of creating support for the new government
   d. opposed because it pandered to people

2. Alexander Hamilton believed that
   a. power belonged to the people
   b. that most people had poor judgment
   c. that the rich were no better than the poor
   d. none of the above

3. Alexander Hamilton
   a. was a financial and political conservative
   b. was forward-looking in his economic programs but politically conservative
   c. believed in free trade but opposed a protective tariff
   d. believed in distributing powers equally to both the executive and legislative branches of government

4. The primary objectives of Hamilton's financial program were
   a. to promote agricultural growth in the West
   b. to establish the country's credit with the French
   c. to promote commercial expansion overseas
   d. all of the above

5. Jefferson believed that
   a. the government should only have powers specifically designated by the Constitution
   b. Hamilton's programs represented a reasonable solution to the new nation's problems
   c. the yeoman farmer and the city artisan were the backbone of the republic
   d. Hamilton's proposal for the bank would hinder the development of commerce and manufacturing

6. The Whiskey Rebellion was incited by
   a. Revolutionary War veterans still angry about taxation without representation
   b. western Federalists jealous of Hamilton's power over Washington
   c. resentful farmers whose livelihood was threatened by the tax on whiskey
   d. tavernkeepers

7. The French Revolution
   a. was a radical social revolution
   b. divided both Europeans and Americans
   c. offered Americans trading opportunities
   d. all of the above

8. The Democratic-Republican societies
   a. supported revolutionary France
   b. supported American neutrality in the European wars
   c. were led by common working people
   d. sought to remove both French and English influence from the United States

9. Jay's Treaty
   a. succeeded in removing the British from western fur-trading posts
   b. resolved almost none of America's grievances with England
   c. provided guarantees against the impressment of American seamen
   d. opened the West Indies to significant American shipping

10. John Adams and Thomas Jefferson
    a. had similar ideas on the role of the national government
    b. were contending for the leadership of the Federalist party
    c. had been enemies from the time of the Continental Congress
    d. had divergent ideas about the development of the new nation

11. The Alien and Sedition Acts
   a. nearly succeeded in squelching Jeffersonian criticism of Federalist policies
   b. were aimed at advocates of a strong navy
   c. were declared unconstitutional by the Supreme Court
   d. were attacked by Jefferson but defended in Madison's Virginia Resolutions

12. The "Revolution of 1800"
   a. was the occasion of the passage of the Bill of Rights
   b. revealed strong sectional divisions
   c. represented yet another Federalist victory
   d. was decided definitively in the electoral college

13. The Federalists
   a. had strong support in the South as well as in the North
   b. had a strong following among agriculturalists
   c. had mainly northern support
   d. were so weak no one supported the party

Essays

1. Compare and contrast the ideological positions and visions of the Federalists and the Jeffersonian Republicans in the 1790s.

2. Analyze and evaluate the reasons for the dominance of Federalist party principles in the 1790s.

3. Explain the reasons for the rise of political parties in the 1790s.

4. Explain the importance of Hamilton's plans for future economic growth.

5. Outline the major difficulties that the French Revolution caused for American foreign policy.

Identify and Interpret: Quotation
(that is, state who, what, where, when, and why significant)

To conclude—Here's success to honest TOM PAINE:
May he live to enjoy what he does well explain.
The just Rights of Man we never forget
For they'll save Britain's friends from the BOTTOMLESS PITT.

"Less respect to the consuming speculator, who wallows in luxury, than to the productive mechanic, who struggles with indigence."

9

Society and Politics in the Early Republic

(1) CHAPTER OUTLINE

Mary and James Harrod carry their children and household possessions away from a difficult life in the Virginia uplands to a more hopeful future in Kentucky. Likewise, two African-Americans, Ben Thompson and Phyllis Sherman, arrive from their former homes to carve out a life in New York's community of free blacks.

Restoring American Liberty
    The Jeffersonians Take Control
    Politics and the Federal Courts
    Dismantling the Federalist War Program

Building an Agrarian Nation
    The Jeffersonian Vision
    The Windfall Louisiana Purchase
    Opening the Trans-Mississippi West

A Nation of Regions
    The Northeast
    The Urban Northeast
    The South
    Trans-Appalachia

Indian-White Relations in the Early Republic
    The Initial Goals of Indian Policy
    Strategies of Survival: The Iroquois and the Cherokee
    Patterns of Armed Resistance: The Shawnee and the Creek

Perfecting a Democratic Society
    The Revolutionary Heritage
    The Evangelical Impulse
    Patterns of Wealth and Poverty
    Alleviating Poverty and Distress
    Women's Lives
    Race, Slavery, and the Limits of Reform

A Foreign Policy for the New Nation
Jeffersonian Principles
Struggling for Neutral Rights
The War of 1812
The United States and the Americas

Politics in Transition
Division Among the Jeffersonians
The Specter of Sectionalism
Collapse of the Federalist-Jeffersonian Party System
A New Style of Politics

Conclusion: The Passing of an Era

(2) SIGNIFICANT THEMES AND HIGHLIGHTS

1. This chapter focuses on the first three decades of the nineteenth century, a period of intense political activity, religious enthusiasm, economic growth, and westward expansion. The chapter emphasizes the attempts of the Jeffersonian Republicans to reshape national political life and to realize their vision of liberty in an agrarian republic.

2. Though the country was politically united, significant regional differences existed between the rural populations of the Northeast, the South, and the Trans-Appalachian West.

3. During the early republic there were numerous efforts to create a distinctive American social order, one that would support the new republican government.

4. The chapter continues the story of Indian-white relations. Between 1790 and 1820, tribal groups developed strategies of accommodation, resistance, and survival. Some tribes, like the Seneca inspired by Handsome Lake, underwent cultural renewal. Others, like the Cherokee, adopted many of the ways of white society. Still others, like the Shawnee and Creek nations, chose armed resistance. At the same time, the federal government developed policies, based on both humanitarian and territorial concerns, that guided Indian-white relations for the rest of the nineteenth century.

5. In the field of foreign affairs, Jeffersonians attempted to fashion policies that would free the nation of entangling alliances with European powers, eliminate foreign troops from American soil, and protect American maritime interests. Although foreign policy measures were in the short run unsuccessful, as the War of 1812 indicated, the United States soon after stated its unique claim to influence the Western Hemisphere.

(3) LEARNING GOALS

Familiarity with Basic Knowledge

After reading this chapter, you should be able to:

1. Explain three measures Jefferson took to reshape and change the federal government.

2. Explain the reasons why Jefferson believed agricultural life was essential to political liberty.

3. Explain the basic features of the different regions in the United States.

4. Show how changing land acts affected settlement of the public domain.

5. Explain the significance of reform efforts and the impact on society.

6. Show the conflicting goals of federal Indian policy.

7. Outline the causes and significance of the War of 1812 and of the Monroe Doctrine.

Practice in Historical Thinking Skills

After reading this chapter, you should be able to:

1. Compare and contrast the survival strategies of the Cherokee, Shawnee, and Creek nations and evaluate how well you think their different strategies worked.

2. Discuss the validity of the American claim that the War of 1812 was the "second War of American Independence."

3. Explain the forces that weakened Jefferson's party.

(4) IMPORTANT DATES AND NAMES TO KNOW

1789	Knox's reports on Indian affairs
1790s	Second Great Awakening begins
1794	Battle of Fallen Timbers (Ohio)
1795	Treaty of Greenville
1796	Congress establishes Indian Factory System
1800	Capital moves to Washington, D.C.

1801	Thomas Jefferson elected president
	Judiciary Act
	New Land Act
1802	Repeal of Judiciary Act
1803	*Marbury* v. *Madison*
	Louisiana Purchase
1803-1806	Lewis and Clark expedition
1803-1812	Napoleonic Wars resume
	British impress American sailors; French seize U.S. vessels
1804	Jefferson reelected
1805-1807	Pike's explorations in the West
1806	Non-Importation Act
1807	*Chesapeake-Leopard* incident
	Embargo Act
	Congress prohibits slave trade
1808	James Madison elected president
	Cherokee legal code established
1809	Tecumseh's confederacy formed
1811	Battle of Kithtippecanoe (Indiana)
1812	War of 1812 with England declared
	Annexation of West Florida
	Madison reelected
1813	Battle of Thames River (Ontario, Canada)
1813-1814	Creek War
1814	Washington, D.C. occupied by British forces
	Hartford Convention convenes
	Treaty of Ghent
	Battle of Horseshoe Bend (Alabama)
1815	Battle of New Orleans
	United States establishes military posts in trans-Mississippi West

| 1816 | James Monroe elected president |
| | Second Bank of the United States chartered |

1819	Transcontinental Treaty (Adams-Onis) with Spain
	Spain cedes East Florida to United States
	McCulloch v. *Maryland*

| 1819-1822 | Bank panic and depression |

1820	Monroe reelected
	Land Act
	Missouri Compromise

| 1822 | Diplomatic recognition of Latin American republics |

| 1823 | Monroe Doctrine proclaimed |

| 1824 | John Quincy Adams elected president |

| 1827 | Cherokees adopt written constitution |

Other Names to Know

| John Ross | Tecumseh | Benjamin Banneker |
| Elskwatawa | Judith Murray | |

(5) GLOSSARY OF IMPORTANT TERMS

full-blooded: term applied to Indians who had only Indian blood to distinguish them from mixed-blooded Indians

War Hawks: a group of Republican leaders, including Clay and Calhoun, who pressed for a warlike stance toward Great Britain and urged territorial expansion into Canada and Florida

(6) ENRICHMENT IDEAS

1. On an outline map of the United States, trace the route of the Lewis and Clark expedition. Fill in the area acquired in the Louisiana Purchase and trace the Transcontinental Treaty Line of 1819 (Adams-Onis). What conclusions do you draw about the relationship between exploration and expansion? Finally, add Florida, New Orleans, and other important battle sites of the War of 1812.

2. Develop a position paper supporting or rejecting war with Great Britain from the point of view of a member of Congress from the South, the West, and New England. What

would be the differences between the positions and specific arguments of the three congressmen?

3. Imagine yourself, like the Harrods, moving into Kentucky or Indiana. Or imagine yourself as Ben Thompson and Phyllis Sherman, free blacks carving out a life in New York. Or imagine yourself a Seneca, Shawnee, or Cherokee young person. In each case, describe your life and feelings.

(7) SAMPLE TEST AND EXAMINATION QUESTIONS

Multiple choice: Choose the best answer.

1. Jeffersonians were initially concerned about all of the following EXCEPT
    a. Federalist officeholders
    b. lame-duck appointments
    c. Adams's proposal for an elected judiciary
    d. the Judiciary Act

2. In the *Marbury v. Madison* decision, Chief Justice Marshall
    a. declared the Maryland law taxing the Second Bank of the United States unconstitutional
    b. declared that the Bank of the United States was unconstitutional
    c. affirmed the principle of exclusive judicial review
    d. all of the above

3. During Jefferson's administration
    a. Federalists were jailed for criticizing Jefferson
    b. the provisional army was dismantled and defense costs lowered
    c. farmers were rewarded for homesteading
    d. the navy built a large fleet to protect U.S. trade

4. The Second Great Awakening's most important impact was:
    a. it encouraged believers to take an interest and perform good works in the community
    b. its message had little meaning for ordinary people
    c. it appealed only to women who found new spiritual strength
    d. it created complex theological ideas

5. Jefferson felt justified in buying the Louisiana Territory
    a. because the Constitution allowed the president to acquire new territories
    b. because he was sure the country approved of his action
    c. because his party pressed him to acquire it
    d. because Napoleon was offering if for less than Jefferson had been prepared to spend

6. The federal government between 1790 and 1820
   a. continued to acquire Native American lands
   b. wanted to protect Indians from unscrupulous exploitation
   c. adopted a new treaty strategy
   d. all of the above

7. The Embargo Act
   a. forbade American ships from sailing to foreign ports
   b. prohibited the importation of English goods
   c. declared impressment illegal
   d. threatened to invoke an embargo on France or England if the other did not cease its violations of American neutral rights on the high seas

8. The most eager calls for war with Great Britain came from
   a. the Federalists
   b. western and southern Republicans
   c. New England merchants
   d. southern planters

9. A distinctive feature of religious practices during the Second Great Awakening was
   a. a meeting with Native American tribal leaders
   b. a meeting of the young War Hawks
   c. the camp meetings
   d. a prayer meeting often held at agricultural fairs

10. The Treaty of Ghent
    a. resolved outstanding American differences with Great Britain
    b. avoided most important areas of dispute
    c. contained an agreement that the British would evacuate western forts
    d. resolved boundary disputes in the Oregon Territory

11. The Monroe Doctrine
    a. was a policy developed by Americans with the aid of British diplomats
    b. was distinctly anti-European in tone
    c. led to immediate American involvement in Latin American affairs
    d. put fear into the hearts of European diplomats

12. The leader of Shawnee political and military resistance was
    a. Tecumseh   c. The Prophet
    b. Sequoyah   d. Handsome Lake

13. Between 1812 and 1828,
    a. the Federalist party collapsed
    b. the Jeffersonian Republicans evolved into a new political party
    c. the Anti-Federalist party collapsed
    d. both (a) and (b) happened

14. After 1812, the government did all of the following EXCEPT
    a. charter the First Bank of the United States
    b. pass the first protective tariff
    c. sponsor internal improvements
    d. stimulate economic expansion

15. When Jefferson said "This momentous question, like a firebell in the night . . . [has] awakened and filled me with terror," he was referring to
    a. the Monroe Doctrine
    b. the Kansas-Nebraska Act
    c. Stono's rebellion
    d. the Missouri Compromise

Essays

1. Write an essay on the following statement: "Once in power, the Jeffersonian Republicans retreated from many of the positions they had held as the opposition party." Show the extent to which you agree with the statement, and support your position with evidence.

2. Write an essay showing the key differences in the geographic regions (Northeast, South, and West).

3. The War of 1812 was not merely a war against an external foe but stemmed from internal problems as well. Write an essay taking this statement as your starting point.

4. Evaluate the survival strategies of several Native American nations and compare them with the foreign policy strategies of the young United States. Which were more successful, and why do you think so?

Identify and Interpret: Quotation
(that is, state who, what, where, when, and why significant)

Let us, then, with courage and confidence pursue our own Federal and Republican principles, our attachment to union and representative government. Kindly separated by nature and a wide ocean from the exterminating havoc of one quarter of the globe; too high-minded to endure the degradations of the others; possessing a chosen country, with room enough for our descendants to the thousandth and thousandth generation; entertaining a due sense of our equal right to the use of our own faculties, to the acquisitions of our own industry, to honor and confidence from our fellow-citizens, resulting not from birth, but from our actions and their sense of them; enlightened by a benign religion, professed, indeed, and practiced in various forms . . . with all these blessings, what more is necessary to make us a happy and a prosperous people?

Still one thing more, fellow-citizens—a wise and frugal Government, which shall restrain men from injuring one another, shall leave them otherwise free to regulate their own pursuits of industry and improvement, and shall not take from the mouth of labor the bread it has earned. This is the sum of good government, and this is necessary to close the circle of our felicities.

Map question:

Locate the following on the accompanying map.

1. Louisiana Territory
2. Spanish East Florida
3. Missouri Compromise Line
4. disputed Oregon Territory
5. Battle of Kithtippecanoe
6. New Orleans
7. Transcontinental Treaty Line of 1819
8. areas inhabited by the Shawnee, Cherokee, and Creek nations
9. Gulf Coast areas added during War of 1812
10. site of Constitutional Convention

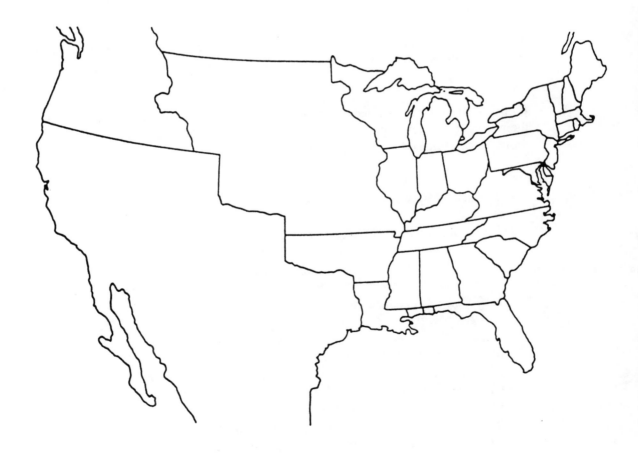

INDUSTRIAL TECHNOLOGY IN THE WOODEN AGE

The decades between 1790 and 1830 witnessed the first stirrings of a revolution in industrial technology that during the rest of the nineteenth century would transform the American economy and shape the working lives of millions of Americans. The nation's earliest experiments in industrial technology were fashioned out of wood, not iron. Though wooden machinery often broke down, required continuous maintenance, and frequently caught fire from friction, it was cheap to construct, easily repaired, and readily fabricated by experienced craftsmen. Wooden machinery, moreover, was especially well suited to the small scale of American manufacturing. The early republic was still part of the "wooden age," when, in addition to tools and machines, wood was the major source of fuel, construction material for ships and wagons, and important chemicals such as potash and turpentine.

Many Americans in the young republic were enthusiastic about technology's promise for the nation's future. Observed Tench Coxe, an ardent promoter of American economic development, "Machines, ingeniously constructed, will give us immense assistance." Robert Fulton, inventor of one of the earliest steamboats, explained how technological progress would strengthen American republicanism. "Every order of things, which has a tendency to remove oppression and meliorate the condition of man, by directing his ambition to useful industry," he proclaimed in a speech before Congress in 1810, "is, in effect, republican." Fulton's comments reflected a widely held belief that technology, representing the practical application of reason and science, would foster human progress. Franklin's lightning rod seemed to sanction that belief. The impact of industrial technology on people's lives, however, was not altogether beneficial.

In 1789, an enterprising immigrant mechanic named Samuel Slater arrived in New York. Familiar with British textile technology, he brought with him detailed knowledge of mechanical carding machines that combed cotton fibers into alignment suitable for spinning and the Arkwright spinning frame, capable of fashioning 48 uniform cotton threads at a time. Powered by waterwheels and placed in the fledgling textile factories that dotted the New England countryside in increasing numbers from the 1790s on, these machines helped spur a startling growth in the American textile industry. In 1800, an estimated 1,000 wage earners labored in the nation's textile factories. By 1830, the number had climbed to 55,000.

Though the new machines increased the output of cotton cloth, they created an unhealthy environment for the workers who tended them. Not only were the early textile factories deafeningly noisy because of the pounding machines and clacking wooden gears, but they were dangerous as well. Cotton dust filled the air, and the leather belts that transmitted power from the factory's waterwheels to the machinery frequently caught workers' hair or clothing, with awful results. Tending the machines, moreover, required repetitious and deadening labor, a fact that led factory managers to fill their work force with children—who were docile and commanded low wages.

Samuel Slater staffed his first factory entirely with youngsters between 7 and 12. By 1820, children comprised an estimated 47 percent of the labor force in Connecticut and 55 percent in Rhode Island. The children's workweek in the Connecticut mills ranged from 72 to 84 hours. In response to such obvious exploitation, the Connecticut legislature passed a law requiring instruction in reading, writing, and arithmetic for all children working in factories. The law, however, simply made child labor more acceptable.

Not until the middle of the nineteenth century would factories replace homes and shops as producers of most American textiles, and it would be another 30 years before most nonagricultural workers spent their days at factory labor. The awesome transformation of manufacturing technology, however, had its beginnings many years earlier, in the primitive wooden machinery of early America.

PART THREE (Chapters 10-16)

AN EXPANDING PEOPLE
1820 - 1877

During the first half of the nineteenth century, a young nation expanded rapidly. As Americans surged west across the Appalachians, secured vast new territories beyond the Mississippi, and, in the 1840s, pushed on to the Pacific Coast, the population soared and became more diverse with the arrival of thousands of immigrants and the inclusion of western Indians and Mexicans. In the East, new modes of production laid the foundation for the material comfort that has come to characterize American life. But expansion sharpened regional differences, particularly between the North and the South, and the period ended with the most devastating conflict the nation has ever experienced.

Chapters 10, 11, and 12 cover roughly the same time period, and each chapter complements the other two. Chapter 10, "Currents of Change in the Northeast and the Old Northwest," investigates the economic and social transformations that affected work, social and family relations, and the rhythms of everyday life in these two regions. Chapter 11, "Slavery and the Old South," considers the South's distinctive economic and social system, which, based as it was on slavery, raised questions about the special virtue of the nation and the meaning of justice, equality, and freedom.

In Chapter 12, "Shaping America in the Antebellum Age," we focus on economic and social changes that sharpened the familiar tension between narrowly defined self-interest and social concerns. Some Americans sought to counteract the selfish tendencies of their age by establishing utopian societies; others tried to preserve ideals and virtue through reform activities or religious experiments. Still others sought to shape their world through politics. The election of Andrew Jackson as president marked the advent of the second American party system and of a lively political culture firmly rooted in new economic and social conditions. Yet while more white Americans than ever were politically active, they disagreed on the competing claims of liberty and power.

Chapter 13, "Moving West," shows the power of American expansionism and the limited meaning many Americans gave to terms like *liberty* and *equality*. During the decade of the 1840s, war and diplomacy won vast new territories, peopled mostly by Mexicans and Native Americans. As settlers to new frontiers sought to re-create familiar institutions and patterns, these earlier inhabitants found themselves excluded from most of the promises of American life.

Territorial expansion not only illustrated questionable environmental practices and the limitations of political and social ideals, but also instigated angry political debates. The expansion of slavery into the West threatened the political balance of power between the North and the South and raised the question of where power and authority lay to decide the future of the West. These questions—which are addressed in Chapters 14, 15, and 16—could not be easily resolved.

Chapter 14, "The Union in Peril," traces the disintegration of the second party system and the eruption of civil war in Kansas. By 1850, two cultures and two societies jostled uneasily in one union, unable to agree on most of the important questions of the day. Secession and civil war soon followed. Chapter 15, "The Union Severed," examines the Civil War and the unanticipated results of the conflict. For example, although the war ended slavery, emancipation itself proved to be problematic. Also unexpected were the transformation of northern and southern society and the new conflicts that emerged. Chapter 16, "The Union Reconstructed," explores how Americans tried to resolve these and the many other dilemmas of the postwar period. With the return of the South to the Union, how would the political system on the local and national level be arranged? What would traditional ideals mean for white southerners, black freedmen, and white northerners?

10

Currents of Change in the Northeast and the Old Northwest

(1) CHAPTER OUTLINE

Susan Warner's privileged and comfortable life is suddenly destroyed when her father loses most of his fortune in the panic of 1837. As Susan searches for ways to help her family, she discovers the economic possibilities of novel writing. Her books attract readers who find her description of the period's economic and social uncertainties convincing.

Economic Growth
> Expansion and Immigration
> Transportation: The Critical Factor
> Capital Investment
> The Role of Government
> The Innovative Mentality
> Ambivalence Toward Change
> The Advance of Industrialization

Early Manufacturing
> The Impact of Industrialization
> A New England Textile Town
> Working and Living in a Mill Town
> Female Responses to Work
> The Changing Character of the Work Force
> Factories on the Frontier

Urban Life
> The Process of Urbanization
> Class Structure in the Cities
> The Urban Working Class
> Middle-Class Life and Ideals
> Mounting Urban Tensions
> The Black Underclass

Rural Communities
> Farming in the East
> Frontier Families
> Opportunities in the Old Northwest

Conclusion: The Character of Progress

(2) SIGNIFICANT THEMES AND HIGHLIGHTS

1. This chapter concentrates on the economic and social transformations in the Northeast and the Midwest between 1820 and 1860. The chapter discusses the factors contributing to economic growth, particularly the importance of changes in transportation, and explores industrialization as a new means of production and as a source of social change. The chapter shows that the process of industrialization was uneven, as old and new ways of production existed side by side.

2. Five types of communities (Lowell; Philadelphia; Cincinnati; Hampshire County, Massachusetts; and the Indiana frontier) are discussed to show how each participated in economic growth. The ways in which different classes, ethnic groups, and races responded to new conditions and shared or failed to share in the benefits of growth are highlighted.

3. The persistence of Revolutionary ideology is evident in working-class critiques of the new industrial world, while new middle-class ideals emerged as a response to changing economic and social conditions.

4. Samuel Breck of Philadelphia is introduced as an example of an upper-class urban dweller. Several mill girls (Mary Paul and Sally Rice) appear at various points in the chapter. The Skinners give an idea of life on the Indiana frontier.

(3) LEARNING GOALS

Familiarity with Basic Knowledge

After reading this chapter, you should be able to:

1. List and explain major factors contributing to economic growth and explain how changes in transportation were of critical importance.

2. Define the term *industrialization* and identify the parts of the United States where industrialization took hold between 1830 and 1860.

3. Define the *cult of domesticity* and explain the reasons for its development and describe new views of childhood.

4. Describe urban class structure and compare it to rural class structure.

5. Explain the process of establishing a family farm on the midwestern frontier.

6. Discuss the contribution of nontangible factors to economic growth.

Practice in Historical Thinking Skills

After reading this chapter, you should be able to:

1. Show how Cincinnati illustrates the uneven process of industrialization and the emergence of new types of work and new workers, and contrast the situation in Cincinnati with the Lowell system.

2. Analyze the ways in which both male and female workers used Revolutionary ideology as a means of criticizing the new work order.

3. Summarize the ways in which economic and social changes affected people's lives both by increasing opportunities and benefits and by separating people from one another.

(4) IMPORTANT DATES AND NAMES TO KNOW

1805	*Palmer* v. *Mulligan*
1815	Waltham textile mills established
1817-1850	Construction of canals in the Northeast
1819	*Dartmouth College* v. *Woodward*
1820	Lowell founded by Boston Associates Land Act of 1820 The term *woman's sphere* becomes current
1824	*Sturges* v. *Crowninshield*
1825	Completion of Erie Canal (Albany to Buffalo, New York)
1825-1856	Construction of canals linking Ohio and Mississippi rivers with the Great Lakes
1828	Baltimore and Ohio Railroad begins operation
1830	Preemption Act
1830s	Boom in the Old Northwest Increasing discrimination against free blacks Public education movement spreads
1833	Philadelphia establishes small police force

1834	Philadelphia race riot
	Lowell work stoppage
	Cyrus McCormick patents reaper
1837	Horace Mann becomes secretary of Massachusetts Board of Education
1837-1844	Financial panic and depression
1840	Agitation for ten-hour day
1840s-1850s	Rising tide of immigration

Other Names to Know

Sarah Hale	Catharine Beecher
Prudence Crandall	

(5) GLOSSARY OF IMPORTANT TERMS

economic growth: an increase in output, usually involving not only expansion but changes in the methods of production

Waltham system: the system of textile production in which all stages of the manufacturing process were brought together

cult of domesticity: set of beliefs insisting that women had different characteristics than men, which made them best suited for the private sphere of home and family

entrepreneur: one who takes the risks of starting new ventures or one who owns or manages one or more businesses

industrial mode of production: the reorganization of production, breaking the process into a series of separate steps done by individual workers or machines

outwork: work done at home or in small shops; workers were usually paid by the piece

(6) ENRICHMENT IDEAS

1. Using the Recovering the Past section as your guide, explore some volumes of early nineteenth-century paintings. What can you discover about the nature of daily life, attitudes, and values from your study?

2. Think how you might write an article for a Cincinnati newspaper evaluating some of the changes in work in the antebellum period if you were the owner of a furniture factory, a widow taking in piecework, or a former cabinetmaker now working in the factory.

3. Write a diary entry for one day in the life of a Lowell mill girl in the 1830s. Give a clear sense of your daily schedule as well as your response to your job and free time. How would your entry differ if you were an Irish girl in the 1850s?

4. If you live in the Midwest, visit the Conner Prairie Settlement near Indianapolis. This living-history museum, which uses first-person interpreters as villagers, conveys a realistic picture of daily life on the frontier in the 1830s. Other living museums can suggest the ways in which rural American life changed in the period before the Civil War.

5. If you live in or near a northeastern, Middle Atlantic, or South Atlantic city, plan a walking tour to the part of the city constructed during the period covered by this chapter. What kinds of buildings date from that era? What were they used for? Are there any examples of housing? What class of persons may have lived in these houses? Are there any remaining evidences of working-class neighborhoods? Visit an early mill complex. What can it tell you about the industrial process, the nature of work, and the reality of life in a mill community?

(7) SAMPLE TEST AND EXAMINATION QUESTIONS

Multiple choice: Choose the best answer.

1. The Lowell work force was typically made up of
   a. older married women
   b. married men
   c. single men
   d. young single women

2. Lowell mill owners constructed boardinghouses for their workers because
   a. they believed workers needed comfortable housing
   b. they wanted to attract a respectable work force
   c. they believed privacy was essential after a long day of toil
   d. they were copying European models

3. In 1840, about what percentage of all Americans lived in cities?
   a. 2 percent
   b. 10 percent
   c. 25 percent
   d. 50 percent

4. Population growth in the early decades of the nineteenth century occurred because of
   a. the increasing size of families
   b. a dramatic drop in death rates
   c. an increase in foreign immigration, mainly from Ireland and Germany
   d. an increase in immigrants from eastern and southern Europe

5. State governments
   a. rarely gave economic entrepreneurs special advantages
   b. levied heavy taxes on business profits
   c. favored farmers
   d. gave loans for internal improvements

6. The courts
   a. were slow to recognize new attitudes toward property
   b. reinforced the notion that business contracts were binding
   c. were lenient toward debtors
   d. none of the above

7. Early textile mills clustered around waterways in
   a. the South
   b. only New England
   c. the Middle Atlantic states
   d. in New England and the Middle Atlantic states

8. The Erie Canal connected
   a. the Great Lakes with New York's Hudson River
   b. the Great Lakes with the Mississippi River
   c. Lake Erie with Lake Ontario
   d. all of the above

9. The composition of the Lowell work force changed because
   a. women got married and therefore did not need the money
   b. women found they could earn more in other jobs
   c. mill owners preferred to hire Irish immigrants, who worked for less
   d. unions successfully organized the mills

10. The cult of domesticity suggested
    a. that while men and women were substantially similar, women belonged in the private sphere
    b. that women should make vital economic contributions to their families
    c. that women's innate differences from men made them suitable only for the private sphere
    d. that women belonged in the public sphere

11. Most Cincinnati workers labored
    a. alone
    b. in small and medium-size shops
    c. in large factories
    d. alongside slaves

12. City services in Philadelphia were provided for
    a. all citizens
    b. all white citizens
    c. all but the Irish
    d. those who could pay for them

13. Between 1830 and 1860,
    a. the gap between the urban rich and the poor narrowed
    b. many of the poor entered the middle class
    c. the gap between rich and poor widened
    d. little changed

14. Rural Americans in the Northeast
    a. had little contact with new economic trends
    b. were born, raised, and died in the same communities
    c. began to change traditional patterns as they came into contact with the industrial world
    d. generally enjoyed social and economic equality

15. Many Americans believed that free public education was important because
    a. they wanted their children to be independent thinkers
    b. it inculcated proper work habits
    c. it promoted social change
    d. it was a good way to keep children off the street

16. Horace Mann was
    a. an educational reformer
    b. an early manufacturer of textiles
    c. an inventor of railroad equipment
    d. a Philadelphia banker

17. Philadelphia had
    a. few blacks compared to other northern cities
    b. no blacks
    c. more blacks than other northern cities
    d. a socially homogeneous black community

Identify and show a relationship between each of the following pairs:

falling birth rates	*and*	new views of childhood
Lowell mills	*and*	Philadelphia
Irish immigration	*and*	frontier farming
Philadelphia race riot	*and*	Lowell work stoppage of 1834
cult of domesticity	*and*	*Dartmouth* v. *Woodward*

Essays

1. Items 1-3 under "Practice in Historical Thinking Skills" in "Learning Goals" suggest topics for practice in essay writing.

2. The life of "intimacy and quietness" was disintegrating in the decades between 1830 and 1860 and was replaced by a life of separateness and clamor. Discuss this statement with appropriate supporting evidence.

Identify and Interpret: Quotation
(that is, state who, what, where, when, and why significant)

Rules and Regulations to be attended to and followed by the Young Persons who come to Board in this House:

Rule first: *Each one to enter the house without unnecessary noise or confusion, and hang up their bonnet, shawl, coat, etc., in the entry.*

Rule second: *Each one to have their place at the table during meals, the two which have worked the greatest length of time in the Factory to sit on each side of the head of the table, so that all new hands will of course take their seats lower down, according to the length of time they have been here.*

Rule third: *It is expected that order and good manners will be preserved at table during meals—and at all other times either upstairs or down.*

Rule fourth: *There is no unnecessary dirt to be brought into the house by the Boarders, such as apple cores or peels, or nut shells, etc.*

Rule fifth: *Each boarder is to take her turn in making the bed and sweeping the chamber in which she sleeps. . . .*

Rule eighth: *The doors will be closed at ten o'clock at night, winter and summer, at which time each boarder will be expected to retire to bed.*

Rule ninth: *Sunday being appointed by our Creator as a Day of Rest and Religious Exercises, it is expected that all boarders will have sufficient discretion as to pay suitable attention to the day, and . . . they will keep within doors and improve their time in reading, writing, and in other valuable and harmless employment.*

THE SEWING MACHINE

In 1860, *Godey's Lady's Book* hailed the sewing machine as the "queen of inventions," crediting it not only with the power to transform the work of American women but also with the ability to "do a hundred times more toward clothing the indigent and feeble than the united fingers of all the [world's] charitable and willing ladies." Like many innovations, the marvelous device was the result of work by several inventors on both sides of the Atlantic. Their interest in a sewing machine was one response to the profusion of manufactured fabrics that were now readily available.

One of the first significant American design breakthroughs came in 1846, when Massachusetts machinist Elias Howe patented a machine with an eyepointed needle and a moving shuttle. Both became standard features of the commercial sewing machine. While Howe was in England trying to sell his machine, Isaac Singer, a onetime mechanic and cabinetmaker, also worked to solve some of the problems connected with the sewing machine, secured a patent in 1851, and began to manufacture and market his machines.

The basic Singer machine was both practical and complex. Special features made the machine relatively easy to operate, but also contributed to its cost. Clothing and shoe manufacturers quickly acquired the machines for their businesses because they could afford to pay the high price and because they recognized their obvious benefits. The introduction of the sewing machine stimulated a period of expansion. By 1858, in the city of Troy, New York, alone, 3,000 machines were turning out men's shirts and collars. Larger and more important than the clothing industry, the shoe industry had an immense demand for sewing machines, the first application of technology to the shoe manufacturing process. By 1860, one female worker, using a machine, was able to stitch together enough shoe uppers to keep 20 shoemakers busy.

Despite their marketing success with clothing and shoe manufacturers, sewing machine makers dreamed of selling their wares to the many thousands of women who were sewing by hand for their families. The sewing machine's purchase price, however, was too high for many family budgets. In 1856, Singer's partner, Edward Clark, came up with the novel idea of allowing buyers to pay for their machines in installments. A woman could put $5 down and pay the rest of the purchase price and interest over several months. The plan succeeded brilliantly. The very next year, sales of Singer machines almost tripled. Clark then hit upon another marketing concept—the trade-in. The Singer Company offered $50 for "old Sewing Machines of any kind" that could be used to finance a new machine. Sales took another leap upward. Profits produced by these innovative schemes allowed improvements in the production of sewing machines that halved prices by 1859.

As sewing machines entered American households, they relieved women of their most time-consuming domestic chore, sewing by hand. Harriet Kidder, the mother of five, welcomed her new "very valuable household article," which made "sewing a pleasure rather than a toil." The calico dress that once demanded over six hours of handsewing now could be finished in less than an hour.

Some women ended up doing more and fancier sewing that they had done without their new machines. If one calico dress took only an hour, why not make several? Ruffles, pleats, tucks, and other embellishments could all be made with the machine, and women's fashions reflected the ornamental possibilities now within reach. Sewing machines also transformed other sewing tasks. Quilting became more elaborate, and many quilters during the second half of the nineteenth century used their machines to create complex works of art.

Many women did not have the luxury of using their machines to sew elaborate clothes or complex quilts. Instead, sewing machines became their means of support. For these women, technology brought a new form of drudgery rather than a liberation from toil. As their experience suggests, technological innovations could have both positive and negative consequences for those who used them.

11

Slavery and the Old South

(1) CHAPTER OUTLINE

Frederick Douglass learns from his masters about complex, intricate chains that bind slaves and masters to each other. He also learns that education is the way to freedom.

Building the Cotton Kingdom
Economic Expansion
White and Black Migrations
The Dependence on Slavery
Slavery and Class in the South
The Nonslaveholding South

Morning: Master in the Big House
The Burdens of Slaveholding
Justifying Slavery

Noon: Slaves in House and Fields
Daily Toil
Slave Health
Slave Law and the Family

Night: Slaves in Their Quarters
Black Christianity
The Power of Song
The Enduring Family

Resistance and Freedom
Forms of Black Protest
Slave Revolts
Free Blacks: Becoming One's Own Master

Conclusion: Douglass's Dream of Freedom

(2) SIGNIFICANT THEMES AND HIGHLIGHTS

1. The tremendous growth of agriculture in the Old South was dependent on cotton and slavery. But contrary to myth, the South was an area of great diversity, regionally,

socially, and in terms of class and slave ownership. These differences bred tensions among whites as well as between masters and slaves.

2. Although slavery was a labor system, the chapter emphasizes the daily life and complex, entangled relationships of white masters and black slaves and points out the difficulties of generalizing about their relationships. The experiences of the family of rice planter Robert Allston suggests some of the dimensions of white slaveholders' lives, while the youth of Frederick Douglass illuminates the lives of black slaves.

3. A unique structure in this chapter discusses slavery in three sections: morning in the Big House, which focuses on white masters; noon in the fields, which looks at daily work and other hardships of the slaves; and nighttime in the quarters, which describes a slave culture and community centered around religion, music, the family, and other adaptive survivals from African culture.

4. Racism was not confined to the South but existed throughout American society. Racism as well as slavery limited black freedom. To a much lesser extent, southern slaveholders also suffered limitations on their freedom from the burdens of the slave system.

(3) LEARNING GOALS

Familiarity with Basic Knowledge

After reading this chapter, you should be able to:

1. Distinguish several geographic regions and the main crops; then describe the socioeconomic class variations of slaveholding patterns in the Old South.

2. Explain the distribution of slaveholders and nonslaveholders in the South.

3. Describe the burdens of slavery from the perspective of the slaveholders and explain five ways in which they justified slavery.

4. Describe a typical day on the plantation for slave men and women, both in the house and in the fields.

5. Explain the nature of black family life and culture in the slave quarters, including how religion, music, and folklore gave the slaves a sense of identity and self-esteem.

6. List five ways in which the slaves protested and resisted their situation.

Practice in Historical Thinking Skills

After reading this chapter, you should be able to:

1. Develop arguments for and against slavery from the perspective of southern slaveholders, nonslaveholding southerners, northern whites, slaves, and freed blacks.

2. Discuss and evaluate the question of who was "free" in southern antebellum society.

3. Identify the author's interpretation of slavery and other possible interpretations.

(4) IMPORTANT DATES AND NAMES TO KNOW

1787	Constitution adopted with proslavery provisions
1793	Eli Whitney invents cotton gin
1800	Gabriel Prosser conspiracy in Virginia
1808	External slave trade prohibited by Congress
1820	South becomes world's largest cotton producer
1822	Denmark Vesey's conspiracy in Charleston
1830s	Southern justification of slavery changes from a necessary evil to a positive good Character of slave system changes Southern laws regulating treatment and manumission of slaves change
1831	Nat Turner's slave revolt in Virginia
1845	*Narrative of the Life of Frederick Douglass* published
1850s	Cotton boom
1851	Indiana state constitution excludes free blacks
1852	Harriet Beecher Stowe publishes best-selling *Uncle Tom's Cabin*
1860	Cotton production and prices peak

Other Names to Know

George Fitzhugh   John Flintoff
Newton Knight   Robert and Adele Allston
Sophia and Hugh Auld

(5) GLOSSARY OF IMPORTANT TERMS

manumission: the freeing of slaves by individual owners

culture: the values and way of life of a group of people that gives the group a unifying identity

polygenesis: the belief that blacks were a separately created race and hence inherently inferior

Herrenvolk democracy: the theory in the antebellum South that although there were economic inequalities among whites, all whites still shared an equality in their superiority to all blacks, a theory that enabled the southern planter elite to minimize class antagonisms among whites

(6) ENRICHMENT IDEAS

1. Find more folktales and stories told by slaves and analyze what they reveal about slave culture. See Harold Courlander, *A Treasury of Afro-American Folklore* (1976) or J. Mason Brewer, *American Negro Folklore* (1968).

2. Listen to some slave spirituals and work songs and analyze them. What do they reveal about the slave experience and about attitudes toward religion? Notice the double meanings.

3. Are there any historical sites in your area related to slavery—for example, plantations, stations on the underground railroad, or slave markets? Do restored plantations give a balanced view of life on the old plantation, the slave quarters as well as the Big House?

4. Consider the heritage of slavery in modern society. To what extent does it still affect our lives and how?

5. Are blacks and whites more or less "free" today than they were during slavery? Are they more or less entangled with each other?

(7) SAMPLE TEST AND EXAMINATION QUESTIONS

Multiple choice: Choose the best answer.

1. Most southern families had
   a. fewer than ten slaves
   b. over ten slaves
   c. no slaves
   d. fewer than five slaves

2. By the 1850s, the largest number of slaves were found in
   a. Texas and Louisiana
   b. the Upper South of Virginia and Kentucky
   c. cities
   d. the black belt stretching from South Carolina across Georgia, Alabama, and Mississippi

3. What percentage of southern white families were slaveholders?
   a. 25 percent
   b. 50 percent
   c. 75 percent
   d. 90 percent

4. The most valuable export crop in the South was
   a. cotton
   b. corn
   c. rice
   d. tobacco

5. The southern economic endeavors with the greatest economic value were
   a. rice and hemp
   b. corn and hogs
   c. cotton and sugarcane
   d. shipbuilding and textiles

6. The typical southern slaveholding family had
   a. fewer than 10 slaves
   b. between 10 and 20 slaves
   c. about 20 slaves
   d. over 50 slaves

7. According to the text, the worst feature of slavery was
   a. the denial of freedom
   b. whippings
   c. the breakup of families
   d. vitamin deficiency and illness

8. The sociological justification of slavery based its argument primarily on
   a. the Bible
   b. the Constitution
   c. scientific assumptions
   d. history

9. After Nat Turner's revolt in 1831, slaves were
   a. more easily given their freedom but treated more harshly
   b. treated less harshly but denied their freedom
   c. feared less than before
   d. given the right to vote

10. Which of the following statements is not true about slave women?
    a. they had networks for mutual support
    b. they were encouraged to have many children
    c. they had no choice in their marriage partners
    d. they sometimes resisted forcible sexual encounters by whites

11. African forms of religious expression
    a. gradually died out in the New World
    b. were too sinful to survive in civilized society
    c. survived in adapted form in the New World
    d. survived in the West Indies but not in the United States

12. The slave family
    a. was destroyed by the slave trade
    b. played a key role in achieving black self-esteem
    c. imitated the family patterns of whites
    d. transmitted black family patterns to whites

13. By the 1850s, the largest number of free blacks were in
    a. the North
    b. the Upper South
    c. the Lower South
    d. Canada

14. We know about the cultural life of slaves in the quarters at night because of
    a. overseers' reports
    b. slave narratives
    c. congressional investigating committees
    d. the diaries of northern visitors

15. Slave culture was expressed most clearly in
    a. songs sung in the fields during the day
    b. Robert Allston's prayer house
    c. religious meetings at night
    d. the incidence of runaways

16. According to the text, a key element for the urban free blacks was
    a. African-American owned business
    b. the likelihood of finding high-paying jobs
    c. African-American churches
    d. the ability to help in numerous slave escapes

Identify and show a relationship between each of the following pairs:

James Hammond	*and*	Newton Knight
Frederick Douglass	*and*	Sophia Auld
yeoman farmers	*and*	poor whites
visible	*and*	invisible black religious institutions
day-to-day resistance	*and*	Nat Turner's revolt

Essays

1. Describe four class levels of southern white society, and show how each might have defended or justified slavery as necessary or good for its self-interest. Which would have defended slavery most vigorously, and why do you think so?

2. Compare and contrast some of the typical events in the daily life of a house slave and a field slave. Which would you have preferred to be and why?

3. Compare and contrast the attitudes of white southerners and white northerners toward blacks. How do you explain whatever differences seem to exist?

4. Describe four or five manifestations of slave culture. Be as specific as you can about sources and modes of expression. Which do you think best expressed authentic slave culture and why?

5. Present an interpretation of slavery from the point of view of three different historians. One sees slavery from the perspective of southern slaveholders, one from the viewpoint of northern white abolitionists, and one from the perspective of the slaves themselves. What would be the major differences?

6. Explain the living conditions and economic circumstances that prevailed for nonslave-holding southern farm families.

12

Shaping America in the Antebellum Age

(1) CHAPTER OUTLINE

Emily and Marius Robinson are separated shortly after their marriage because of their ardent commitment to abolish slavery and to educate free blacks. Despite suffering many hardships of separation, sickness, and mob attack, they persist for a time in an effort to shape and reform American society.

Religious Revival and Reform Philosophy
> Finney and the Second Great Awakening
> The Transcendentalists

The Political Response to Change
> Changing Political Culture
> Jackson's Path to the White House
> Old Hickory's Vigorous Presidency
> Jackson's Indian Policy
> Jackson's Bank War and "Van Ruin's" Depression
> The Second American Party System

Perfectionist Reform and Utopianism
> The Dilemmas of Reform
> Utopian Communities: Oneida and the Shakers
> Other Utopias
> Millerites and Mormons

Reforming Society
> Temperance
> Health and Sexuality
> Humanizing the Asylum
> Working-Class Reform

Abolitionism and Women's Rights
> Tensions Within the Antislavery Movement
> Flood Tide of Abolitionism
> Women's Rights

Conclusion: Perfecting America

(2) SIGNIFICANT THEMES AND HIGHLIGHTS

1. The social and economic changes of the 1830s were both promising and unsettling. This chapter explores the question of how people (both ordinary and prominent) sought to maintain some sense of control over their lives in the 1830s and 1840s. Some, like the Robinsons, poured their energies into reform. Others turned to politics, religion, and new communal lifestyles in order to shape their changing world.

2. Throughout the chapter, social, political, cultural, and economic topics are interrelated and seen as a whole. The chapter merges two major events—democratic Jacksonian politics and the many forms of perfectionist social reform. They began from distinctly different points of view but in fact shared more in common than has usually been recognized.

3. The explanation of politics in the age of Jackson looks at the social and ethnocultural basis of politics, while the analysis of revivalism, religion, and utopian communitarianism stresses the socioeconomic basis of these cultural phenomena.

4. The timeless dilemmas and problems of reformers, especially of temperance, abolitionist, and feminist reformers, are a sub-theme running through the chapter.

(3) LEARNING GOALS

Familiarity with Basic Knowledge

After reading this chapter, you should be able to:

1. Explain the connection between religious revivalism and reform efforts to erase social evils.

2. Describe three ways in which political culture changed between the early 1820s and 1840.

3. Explain the key events and significance of the three major issues in Jackson's presidency—the tariff, the war against the bank, and Indian removal.

4. List and explain the leaders, principles, programs, and sources of support of the two major parties, Democrats and Whigs.

5. List several evils that Americans wanted to reform in the 1830s and 1840s and the major influences that contributed to the reform impulse.

6. Describe some of the purposes, patterns, and problems that most utopian communities shared.

7. Describe the major goals, tactics, and problems in the antebellum reform movements for temperance, abolitionism, and women's rights.

Practice in Historical Thinking Skills

After reading this chapter, you should be able to:

1. Analyze how Jacksonian politicians and social reformers both opposed one another and had much in common.

2. Explain how the changing numbers and composition of voters affected the political structure.

3. Explain the development of the second American party system, showing how it evolved from and differed from the first party system.

4. Understand and explain why people turn to politics, or to religion and revivalism, or to utopian communitarianism, or to specific issue reforms in order to shape their world; and then explain how well these seemed to work.

(4) IMPORTANT DATES AND NAMES TO KNOW

1824	New Harmony established (Indiana)
1825	John Quincy Adams elected president
1826	American Temperance Society founded
1828	Calhoun publishes *Exposition and Protest* Andrew Jackson elected president Tariff of Abominations
1828-1832	Rise of workingmen's parties
1829	David Walker's *Appeal*
1830	Webster-Hayne debate and Jackson-Calhoun toast *The Book of Mormon* published by Joseph Smith Indian Removal Act
1830-1831	Charles Finney's religious revivals
1831	Garrison begins publishing *The Liberator*
1832	Nullification crisis Jackson reelected; Calhoun resigns as vice-president Bank War and Jackson's veto *Worcester* v. *Georgia*
1833	Force Bill and Compromise tariff Removal of deposits from U.S. Bank to state banks begun American Anti-Slavery Society established

1834	New York Female Moral Reform Society founded National Trades Union founded Whig party established
1835-1836	Increasing incidents of mob violence
1836	Gag rule Specie circular Martin Van Buren elected president
1837	Financial panic and depression begin Sarah Grimké's *Letters on the Equality of the Sexes* Emerson's "American Scholar" address
1837-1838	Cherokee "Trail of Tears"
1840	William Henry Harrison elected president American Anti-Slavery Society splits World Anti-Slavery Convention Ten-hour day for federal employees
1840-1841	Transcendentalists found Hopedale and Brook Farm in Massachusetts
1843	Dorothea Dix's report on treatment of the insane Henry Highland Garnet's call for slave rebellion
1844	Joseph Smith murdered in Nauvoo, Illinois
1846-1848	Mormon migration to Great Basin under leadership of Brigham Young
1847	First issue of Frederick Douglass's abolitionist newspaper *North Star*
1848	Noyes founds Oneida community (New York) First women's rights convention at Seneca Falls, New York
1850	Nathaniel Hawthorne's *Scarlet Letter* published
1851	Maine prohibition law Herman Melville's *Moby Dick* published
1853	Children's Aid Society established in New York City
1854	Thoreau publishes *Walden*
1855	Massachusetts bans segregated public schools

Other Names to Know

Henry Clay	Daniel Webster
Nicholas Biddle	Alexis de Tocqueville
Charles G. Finney	Mother Ann Lee
Robert Owen	Joseph Smith
William Miller	Abby Kelley
Elizabeth Cady Stanton	Theodore Dwight Weld
Sylvester Graham	Lucretia Mott

(5) GLOSSARY OF IMPORTANT TERMS

Whigs: party opposing Jackson ("King Andrew I"), their name referring to the English parliamentary party opposed to royal power

nullification: the states' rights doctrine presented by John C. Calhoun of South Carolina which said that a state could declare federal legislation null and void

ethnocultural politics: the belief that political participation and behavior are affected by one's religious, ethnic, and cultural background

millennialism: the religious belief that a thousand-year era (millennium) of perfect peace, harmony, and brotherhood was a prerequisite for the Second Coming of Christ

perfectionism: the religious belief that sin and evil could be eradicated in American society as well as in individuals

transcendentalism: belief of New England intellectuals that the truths found beyond sense experience in intuition and nature would lead people to self-knowledge and self-reliance and ultimately to the attempted reformation of themselves and society

communitarianism: the creation of utopian communities in which members engaged in various forms of cooperation and sharing of property and responsibility for the well-being of all

spiritualism: psychic phenomenon of the 1830s and 1840s by which humans believed they could communicate with unknown worlds, including the dead

abolitionists: reformers who wanted to end slavery

immediatists: abolitionist disciples of Garrison and Weld who wanted to end slavery immediately

nonresistance: the philosophical pacifist belief opposing all forms of governmental or personal coercion

(6) ENRICHMENT IDEAS

1. After reading the Recovering the Past section, find and read foreign visitors' accounts of life in the United States in the 1830s and 1840s. How accurate do you think they were? How would you write about another culture you have seen (or imagined)? What questions would you ask? What limitations would you feel? What cultural assumptions would you bring to your observations?

2. Visit the site of one of the several utopian communities mentioned in the chapter. Many still exist, some even restored as living historical museums. Depending on where you live, you might visit Hopedale or Brook Farm near Boston, Massachusetts; Shaker Villages near Pittsfield, Massachusetts and in Kentucky; Ephrata, Pennsylvania; Zoar, Ohio; New Harmony, Indiana; the Amana colonies in Iowa, etc. Whether or not you can actually visit the original site, you can research further into one or two particular utopian communities.

3. Imagine yourself as part of the colony. How well would you fit in? What would you like and dislike about life in this community? Write a letter to a friend about it, or write a series of imaginary diary entries about life in the community.

4. You can think about similar questions when visiting other sites, for example, Seneca Falls, or Mormon landmarks in Utah, or a prison asylum built in the mid-nineteenth century. A letter or diary entry could be written about your imagined participation in a Whig campaign picnic in 1840, or a revival or temperance meeting broken up by a mob, or a meeting of Mormons considering migration westward, or your presence at the women's rights convention in Seneca Falls.

5. Prepare a diagram showing the development of the American political party system from the 1790s to 1840—specifically party names, leaders, principles, programs, campaign issues, and sources of popular electoral support.

(7) SAMPLE TEST AND EXAMINATION QUESTIONS

Multiple choice: Choose the best answer.

1. The Whig party stood for all of the following programs EXCEPT
    a. a strong national bank
    b. a protective tariff
    c. the right of nullification
    d. restrictions on Sunday business and drinking

2. Which of the following statements best describes the tone of Jackson's presidency?
   a. the emergence of common people to responsibility in government
   b. strong presidential leadership on issues and positions of personal importance to Jackson
   c. unyielding presidential leadership to the principles long clearly identified with the Democratic party
   d. negative leadership, relying on the "kitchen cabinet" to run most executive affairs

3. Jackson defeated John Quincy Adams in 1828 because
   a. Clay's candidacy split the votes Adams should have received
   b. Adams was such an intellectual that the voters did not understand him
   c. voters were so outraged at the attacks on Rachel Jackson that many voted against Adams
   d. Jackson carefully prepared for the election, building a sectionally diverse coalition of support

4. Jacksonian Democrats
   a. supported the concentration of economic power in new corporations
   b. opposed federal government support for public education
   c. were basically advocates of national rather than state sovereignty
   d. encouraged abolitionist criticisms of slavery

5. The Jacksonian era was noteworthy for which change in political practice?
   a. fewer men participated by voting
   b. party organization helped to promote a more democratic style
   c. women began to vote in state elections
   d. only wealthy people could afford to run for office

6. The U.S. Bank performed all of the following services EXCEPT
   a. shifting government funds to different parts of the country
   b. moderating and regulating state banking activities
   c. issuing large quantities of paper money to stimulate purchasing power
   d. buying and selling government bonds

7. The nullification crisis was resolved when
   a. Jackson sent federal troops to Charleston
   b. popular support for Jackson's threat of force and the compromise tariff isolated South Carolina
   c. Calhoun apologized and resigned as vice-president
   d. Van Buren secured passage of the Tariff of Abominations

8. The removal of the Cherokee Indians was justified by all of the following EXCEPT
   a. Jackson's argument that the Cherokee could not survive living among whites
   b. Jackson's argument that they were subject to Georgia state laws
   c. John Marshall's argument that the Indian's case was "repugnant to the Constitution"
   d. white Georgians' arguments that they needed more land for cotton

9. Which one did not support the Whig party?
   a. New England
   b. small Catholic farmers
   c. temperance and other moralistic reformers
   d. large cotton planters with a national vision

10. The primary cause of the reform impulse in America in the 1830s was
    a. the influx of Catholic European immigrants
    b. religious revivalism and socioeconomic changes
    c. northern opposition to slavery
    d. an outpouring of new books describing Biblical scriptures

11. The Finney revivals were characterized by
    a. the idea that ministers were agents who could cause a revival
    b. the idea that revivals were signs of divine intervention
    c. extensive drinking during the lengthy meetings
    d. an emphasis on reason in seeing one's way to conversion

12. Utopian communities collapsed for all of the following reasons EXCEPT
    a. individualism
    b. poor leadership and admissions policies
    c. external hostility
    d. diversified economies

13. Black and white abolitionists
    a. did not work well together because of white paternalism
    b. supported each other well despite occasional disagreements
    c. worked together only in battling race discrimination in the North but not slavery in the South
    d. ignored each other because of the fear of mob violence

14. Which one was not a concern of the women's rights movement in the 1840s?
    a. the right to vote
    b. the right of free speech
    c. better working conditions
    d. equal pay for equal work

15. Temperance reformers
    a. focused exclusively on the moral suasion tactic that drinking was a sin
    b. were split between advocates of moderation and total abstinence
    c. succeeded in passing a prohibition amendment before the Civil War
    d. were led by women who hoped to leave abusive husbands

Matching:

Match the person in column A with the appropriate religious or reform concern in column B.

A	B
____1. Dorothea Dix	a. antislavery and women's rights
____2. William Miller	b. Oneida colony
____3. Abby Kelley	c. public education
____4. Theodore Dwight Weld	d. Shakers
____5. David Ruggles	e. treatment of the insane
____6. Martin Delany	f. abolitionism and temperance
____7. Ralph Waldo Emerson	g. excessive federal power
____8. Horace Mann	h. secular utopian communities
____9. Sylvester Graham	i. black nationalist colonization
___10. Joseph Smith	j. northern racial discrimination
___11. John H. Noyes	k. *Walden*
___12. Robert Owen	l. Second Coming of Christ
___13. Ann Lee	m. diet and sexual restraint
___14. Henry David Thoreau	n. self-reliance
___15. John C. Calhoun	o. Mormonism

Essays

1. Trace the changing development of the American political party system (and political culture) from 1824 to 1840.

2. Discuss the various dilemmas and problems of reformers, with specific references to the temperance, abolitionist, and women's rights movements.

3. Show the relationship between women's rights and abolitionism.

4. Discuss both the differences and the similarities of Jacksonian politics and social reform.

5. Discuss the many reasons why Americans in the 1830s turned to religion, revivalism, utopianism, and reform. Which approach do you think brought individuals the most satisfaction that they had effectively reshaped their world? Did any? Support your essay with evidence from the chapter.

Identify and Interpret: Quotation
(that is, state who, what, where, when, and why significant)

The history of mankind is a history of repeated injuries and usurpations on the part of man toward woman, having in direct object the establishment of an absolute tyranny over her. To prove this, let facts be submitted to a candid world.

He has never permitted her to exercise her inalienable right to the elective franchise.

He has compelled her to submit to laws, in the formation of which she had no voice.

He has withheld from her rights which are given to the most ignorant and degraded men—both natives and foreigners.

Identify and Interpret: Chart

(that is, first, study the chart and describe what it shows; second, analyze the chart by explaining some of the reasons behind the patterns you see; third, assess the larger significance of the chart)

Public Land Sales, 1820-1860

111

13

Moving West

(1) CHAPTER OUTLINE

Lewis Cass presents an optimistic picture of what the westward movement represented for the nation. The experiences of Henry Judah and Thomas Gibson in the Mexican War suggest the underside of westward expansion, as do Mary Gibson's worried letters to her husband.

Probing the Trans-Mississippi West
Foreign Claims and Possessions
Traders, Trappers, and Cotton Farmers
Manifest Destiny

Winning the Trans-Mississippi West
Annexing Texas, 1845
War with Mexico, 1846-1848
California and New Mexico
The Treaty of Guadalupe Hidalgo, 1848
The Oregon Question, 1844-1846

Going West
The Emigrants
Migrants' Motives
The Overland Trails

Living on the Frontier
The Agricultural Frontier
The Mining Frontier
The Mormon Frontier
The Urban Frontier

Cultures in Conflict
Confronting the Plains Tribes
The Fort Laramie Council, 1851
Overwhelming the Mexicans

Conclusion: Fruits of Manifest Destiny

(2) SIGNIFICANT THEMES AND HIGHLIGHTS

1. As the contrasting views of Lewis Cass, Henry Judah, and the Gibsons make clear, the story of the trans-Mississippi West in the nineteenth century is not just the story of the acquisition of territory but also of the experience of thousands of ordinary citizens who fought for new lands or who migrated to the frontier.

2. The chapter emphasizes the use of personal documents, especially the diaries written by men and women on the Overland Trail, in reconstructing historical realities.

3. The political and military events that led to the successful acquisition of western lands came at the expense of Native Americans and Mexicans. The events of this period are presented not only through the eyes of white emigrants but also from the perspective of these two groups.

4. Lewis Cass's attitudes and ideas exemplify the point of view and rhetoric of expansionists who advocated the acquisition of new territories.

(3) LEARNING GOALS

Familiarity with Basic Knowledge

After reading this chapter, you should be able to:

1. Define Manifest Destiny.

2. List the sequence of events resulting in the acquisition of Texas, New Mexico, California, and Oregon. Locate on a map and date the major territorial acquisitions of the United States between 1803 and 1853.

3. Describe the typical emigrant and three motives leading to the decision to migrate to the Far West.

4. List four ways in which white emigration affected the livelihood of Plains Indians.

5. Explain the terms of the Laramie Council agreements and assess their impact on red-white relations.

6. Contrast the experience of Mexican-Americans in Texas, New Mexico, and California.

Practice in Historical Thinking Skills

After reading this chapter, you should be able to:

1. Discuss the United States's policies toward the Plains Indians, placing those events in the context of Indian-white relations until the early 1850s.

2. Compare and contrast opportunities on the mining and farming frontiers.

3. Analyze the role of men and women on the Overland Trail.

(4) IMPORTANT DATES AND NAMES TO KNOW

1803-1806	Lewis and Clark expedition
1818	U.S.-British treaty on joint occupation of Oregon
1819	Spain cedes Florida to the United States and sets transcontinental boundary of the Louisiana Purchase, excluding Texas
1821	Mexican independence from Spain Opening of Santa Fe Trail Stephen Austin leads American settlement of Texas
1821-1840	Indian removals
1829	Georgia revokes Cherokee rights
1830	Mexico abolishes slavery in Texas
1836	Texas declares independence Battles of the Alamo and San Jacinto
1840s	Emigrant crossings of Overland Trail
1844	James Polk elected president
1845	Term *Manifest Destiny* coined United States annexes Texas and sends troops to the Rio Grande; attempts to buy Upper California and New Mexico
1846	Mexico declares defensive war United States declares war and takes Santa Fe Resolution of Oregon boundary question
1847	Attack on Veracruz and Mexico City Mormon migration to Utah begins
1848	Treaty of Guadalupe Hidalgo
1849	California gold rush begins

1850	California admitted to Union
1851	Fort Laramie Treaty
1853	Gadsden Purchase
1862	Homestead Act

Other Names to Know

Sam Houston   Antonio López de Santa Anna
Zachary Taylor   John Slidell
Nicholas Trist

(5) GLOSSARY OF IMPORTANT TERMS

Manifest Destiny: the belief in the political, religious, and cultural superiority of American civilization, giving Americans an inherent right to the continent and "true title" to its lands

emigrant: term used to describe Americans moving to western frontiers

polygamy: a form of marriage in which a husband has more than one wife; believed by nineteenth-century Mormons to be divinely sanctioned

(6) ENRICHMENT IDEAS

1. The Recovering the Past section gives examples of diaries and personal documents written on the Overland Trail and suggests that men and women differed in the content and style of what they wrote in their diaries and journals. Many diaries have been collected and published. Read some of them. What seem to be the typical daily concerns of men? Of women? What can you conclude about the nature of trail life? What work was involved in moving west? What can you learn about family and social life through the diaries? Finally, do you find differences between journals written by men and those written by women? How do you connect these materials with the cult of domesticity and the idea of separate spheres for men and women?

2. The letters of many of the young men who participated in the gold rush are found in printed collections. Some may also be on file with your local historical society, as the men wrote letters to friends and family at home. What picture of mining life can you form from these personal documents? How much opportunity was there in the mining West as reflected in these letters? Did the writers have reasonable expectations of their future? What can you tell about family life and the social character of mining life through reading the letters?

3. In some parts of the United States (Alaska, the West), a later frontier period is still fresh in the memories of older residents. This provides an excellent opportunity for an oral history.

4. On an outline map of the United States, draw in and date the major territorial acquisitions between 1803 and 1853 and the major overland trails and important junctions.

(7) SAMPLE TEST AND EXAMINATION QUESTIONS

Multiple choice: Choose the best answer.

1. Which of the following groups is not matched with the appropriate area?
   a. Five Civilized Tribes and the Oklahoma Territory
   b. settlers and squatters and Texas
   c. fur trappers and traders and the Rocky Mountain region
   d. New England shippers and New Mexico

2. The expression *Manifest Destiny* refers to
   a. the title of a journal published in the 1840s
   b. a speech made by Lewis Cass
   c. the Puritan belief of the uniqueness of the American experience
   d. a belief that because of the superiority of its institutions, Americans should control the North American continent

3. The Transcontinental Treaty of 1819
   a. clearly indicated that Texas belonged to the United States
   b. excluded Texas as part of the United States
   c. made clear that Texas had been part of the Louisiana Purchase
   d. clearly included Oregon as belonging to the United States

4. The Mexican government invited American settlers to Texas
   a. because they feared Texas was weak and needed settlers
   b. because they wanted to gain converts for the Catholic church
   c. because they hoped to see the introduction of American law in this area
   d. because they wanted the labor of black slaves there

5. Texas did not join the Union in 1837
   a. because Texans were still fighting the Mexicans for their independence
   b. because Texans wished to have their own independent republic
   c. because many northerners, fearful of the expansion of slavery, opposed annexation
   d. because Jackson refused to take the advice of his "kitchen cabinet"

6. Polk's objectives in the conflict with Mexico included
   a. obtaining California
   b. obtaining New Mexico
   c. settling the boundary of Texas at the Rio Grande
   d. all of the above

7. The war with Mexico
   a. was complicated by the Oregon question
   b. was clearly Mexico's fault
   c. ended in 1848
   d. was popular throughout the United States

8. The acquisition of the Oregon country gave the United States land in the Northwest
   a. up to the line 54° 40' north latitude
   b. up to the 49th parallel
   c. around San Francisco
   d. all of the above

9. Most overland emigrants traveled
   a. with strangers
   b. with relatives and friends
   c. with people of their own religion
   d. alone

10. The overland trip to Oregon
    a. was so expensive that only the rich could go west
    b. was so cheap that virtually anyone could become an emigrant
    c. cost a substantial amount, making the trip possible only for middle-class Americans
    d. cost far more than making the trip by sea

11. On the mining frontier
    a. most miners struck it rich
    b. most people expected to make a fortune and build expensive houses in the West
    c. miners who failed to get rich quick soon became wage earners
    d. prostitutes were courteously treated because there were so few women

12. In Utah
    a. most families were polygamous
    b. Mormon men usually had more than two wives
    c. polygamous wives frequently tried to escape
    d. few families practiced polygamy

13. The Native Americans of the Great Plains
   a. fiercely attacked the emigrants from the beginning
   b. at first fought one another as much as they did white emigrants
   c. provided buffalo barbecues for emigrants passing through their lands
   d. saw no threat from white emigration

14. All of the following are true about the Fort Laramie Council EXCEPT that it
   a. drew tribal boundaries
   b. secured promises from some of those present to stay within tribal boundaries
   c. succeeded in firmly establishing the reservation policy
   d. gave Native Americans presents and other forms of compensation

15. The Treaty of Guadalupe Hidalgo
   a. assured former Mexicans that they would enjoy the rights of citizens
   b. promised the protection of their property
   c. seemed to legitimate land grants made by Mexico
   d. all of the above

Identify and show a relationship between each of the following pairs:

mining frontier	*and*	bandidos
Fort Laramie Council	*and*	"fifty-four forty or fight"
Manifest Destiny	*and*	the Trail of Tears
Treaty of Guadalupe Hidalgo	*and*	Lewis Cass
Overland Trail	*and*	the Homestead Act

Essays

1. "Manifest Destiny was a policy for whites only." Discuss with specific evidence to support your main points.

2. Although the westward movement may not have realized dreams of opportunity, the fact of emigration did help keep American ideals alive. Write an essay either agreeing or disagreeing with the statement.

3. Analyze the myths and realities of popular images of the American West, specifically in regard to Native Americans and Hispanics.

4. Explain the role that religious attitudes had on the settlement of the West. In what specific cases was it strongest?

Map Question

Locate the following on the accompanying map.

1. The Trail of Tears
2. Oregon and California trails
3. Texas Republic, 1836-1845
4. Sioux and Cheyenne lands
5. Sutter's Fort, California
6. Mormon Trail's end, Salt Lake City
7. Rio Grande
8. Colorado River
9. Territory acquired under the
   Treaty of Guadalupe Hidalgo, 1848

10. Gadsden Purchase
11. Santa Fe Trail
12. Oregon country acquisition, 1846
13. San Francisco
14. Hopi and Navaho lands
15. Black belt
16. Erie Canal

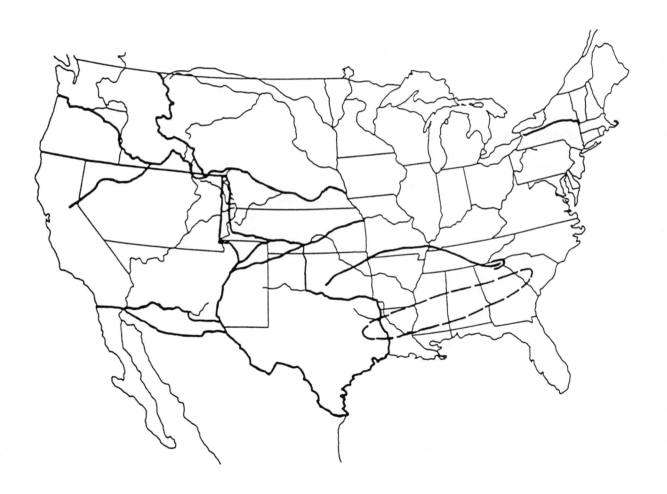

14

The Union in Peril

(1) CHAPTER OUTLINE

As Abraham Lincoln awaits the election returns in November 1860, three other Americans—Robert Allston, a South Carolina slave owner; Frederick Douglass, an escaped slave; and Michael Luark, an Iowa farmer—also watch the results of the election, each filled with intense concern over how the fate of the nation would affect his own.

Slavery in the Territories
> Free Soil or Constitutional Protection?
> Popular Sovereignty and the Election of 1848
> The Compromise of 1850
> Consequences of Compromise

Political Disintegration
> The Apathetic Election of 1852
> The Kansas-Nebraska Act
> Expansionist "Young America"
> Nativism, Know-Nothings, and Republicans

Kansas and the Two Cultures
> Competing for Kansas
> "Bleeding Kansas"
> Northern Views and Visions
> The Southern Perspective

Polarization and the Road to War
> The Dred Scott Case, Kansas, and the Democrats
> Lincoln and the Illinois Debates
> John Brown's Raid
> The Election of 1860

The Divided House Falls
> Secession and Uncertainty
> Lincoln and Fort Sumter

Conclusion: The "Irrepressible Conflict"

(2) SIGNIFICANT THEMES AND HIGHLIGHTS

1. The heightened tensions surrounding the 1860 election and suggested by the anecdote indicate the central place the Civil War occupies in American history. The causes of the war that dissolved the Union, therefore, are crucial to an understanding of America's history. The causes reflect the interrelationship of politics, emotions, and sectional culture.

2. Historians have long debated, without resolution, the causes of the Civil War. This chapter focuses on four developments of the period between 1848 and 1861, each an important cause of war. The chapter weaves these developments together in an interpretive narrative account of both the events and the cultural values behind the events. The student is left to decide how the four causes interacted to bring about the war and which, if any, were more important than others.

3. Events in Kansas in 1855 and 1856 are highlighted as a specific microscopic illustration bringing together many of the forces that led Americans to secession and civil war in 1861.

4. The primary focus in this chapter is on national political developments involving nationally known figures because the Civil War was, after all, fundamentally a political event. Nevertheless, the chapter includes the comments of ordinary Americans, most frequently those of two figures from earlier chapters, runaway slave Frederick Douglass and South Carolina rice planter Robert Allston, as they observed the events of the 1850s leading to the outbreak of civil war.

(3) LEARNING GOALS

Familiarity with Basic Knowledge

After reading this chapter, you should be able to:

1. Explain four proposals for dealing with the territories acquired in the Mexican War and the four provisions of the Compromise of 1850.

2. Describe the breakdown of political parties in the early 1850s, explaining the disappearance of old parties and the emergence of new ones.

3. Outline the course of the Kansas-Nebraska Act and how it affected politics and sectional animosities in the mid-1850s.

4. Explain America's expansionist interest in Latin America.

5. Show how the events in Kansas in 1855 and 1856, the Dred Scott case, the emotional events of 1859-1860, and the election of Lincoln led to the secession crisis and the outbreak of the Civil War.

Practice in Historical Thinking Skills

After reading this chapter, you should be able to:

1. Describe the differing cultural values of the South and North and each section's view of the other, and explain how these cultural differences helped lead to civil war.

2. Explain the development and significance of each of the four causes of the Civil War, citing four or five specific examples for each.

3. Evaluate the four causes, indicating which ones (or one) you think were most significant in explaining why the North and South went to war in 1861.

(4) IMPORTANT DATES AND NAMES TO KNOW

1820	Missouri Compromise
1832	South Carolina nullification crisis
1835-1840	Intensification of abolitionist attacks on slavery Violent retaliatory attacks on abolitionists
1840	Liberty party formed
1846	Wilmot Proviso
1848	Free-Soil party founded Zachary Taylor elected president
1850	Compromise of 1850, including Fugitive Slave Act
1850-1854	"Young America" movement
1851	Women's rights convention in Akron, Ohio
1852	Harriet Beecher Stowe publishes best-selling *Uncle Tom's Cabin* Franklin Pierce elected president
1853	Gadsden Purchase
1854	Ostend Manifesto Kansas-Nebraska Act nullifies Missouri Compromise Formation of Republican and Know-Nothing parties
1855	Walt Whitman publishes *Leaves of Grass*

1855-1856	Julia Lovejoy, David Atchison, and thousands of others pour into Kansas, creating months of turmoil and violence
1856	John Brown's massacre in Kansas Sumner-Brooks incident in U.S. Senate, Washington James Buchanan elected president
1857	Dred Scott decision legalizes slavery in territories Lecompton constitution in Kansas
1858	Lincoln-Douglas debates in Illinois
1859	John Brown's raid at Harpers Ferry (Virginia)
1860	Democratic party splits Four-party campaign Abraham Lincoln elected president
1860-1861	Secession of seven southern states
1861	Confederate States of America founded Attack on Fort Sumter begins Civil War

Other Names to Know

Sojourner Truth	Stephen Douglas
William Walker	Frederick Douglass
William Marcy	William Seward

(5) GLOSSARY OF IMPORTANT TERMS

popular sovereignty: the doctrine that left the decision whether a state would enter the Union slave or free up to the territorial legislature representing the people of that territory

nativism: antiforeign feelings and behavior (especially against Irish Catholic immigrants) expressed by native-born Americans

Young America: a term describing proud, confident, highly nationalistic, expansionist Americans in the early 1850s

(6) ENRICHMENT IDEAS

1. After reviewing the Recovering the Past section, read further into the Senate debates over the Compromise of 1850, analyzing and discussing the style and arguments of various speeches, especially the complete texts of those by Clay, Webster, Calhoun, and Seward.

2. It is 1855. Create a dialogue between two recent migrants to Kansas, one from Massachusetts and one from Missouri. Put them in an appropriate setting and provide an end to their conversation, but focus mainly on how each reveals his or her sectional origins and views and how each sees the other.

3. You are Lincoln in the winter of 1860-1861. What would you do? You are Frederick Douglass in the same winter. What would you do? You are Robert Allston at the same time. What would you do? Why? What do you think would happen?

(7) SAMPLE TEST AND EXAMINATION QUESTIONS

Multiple choice: Choose the best answer.

1. According to the textbook, the most pervasive underlying cause of the Civil War was
    a. slavery
    b. political blundering
    c. abolitionist agitation
    d. economic differences

2. The Wilmot Proviso stated that
    a. Congress should protect slavery in the territories acquired from Mexico
    b. the people of those territories should decide for themselves whether to permit slavery
    c. slavery should be prohibited in territories acquired from Mexico
    d. slavery should be prohibited only north of the line 36°30'

3. The Compromise of 1850 included all of the following provisions EXCEPT
    a. a stronger Fugitive Slave Act
    b. the admission of California as a free state
    c. the abolition of slavery and the slave trade in the District of Columbia
    d. the organization of New Mexico and Utah according to the principle of popular sovereignty

4. Of those blacks arrested in the North under the Fugitive Slave Act, most
    a. were able to purchase their freedom
    b. were returned to the South
    c. escaped and fled to Canada
    d. were rescued by sympathetic whites

5. Central to the nativist fears was
   a. the growing power of slaveholders
   b. a dislike of anyone who favored abolitionism
   c. a hatred of the wealthy
   d. loathing of the Roman Catholic church

6. Party distinctiveness and loyalty decreased in the early 1850s because of
   a. improving economic conditions
   b. the upsurge of expansionist fervor
   c. Fillmore's friendship with Douglas
   d. the lasting success of the Compromise of 1850

7. The Kansas-Nebraska Act
   a. settled the question of slavery in the territories
   b. unified the Democratic party
   c. guaranteed Douglas the presidential nomination in 1856
   d. seriously weakened Douglas's support from northern Democrats

8. The Know-Nothing party advocated
   a. a lengthy period before immigrants could become citizens
   b. the abolition of slavery
   c. government regulation of Catholic parochial schools
   d. all of the above

9. The Republican party in 1860
   a. stood for the principle of popular sovereignty
   b. opposed the extension of slavery into the territories
   c. advocated the abolition of slavery
   d. promised not to interfere with southern slavery but supported equal rights for free blacks in the North

10. Which of the following is in the correct chronological order?
    a. Kansas-Nebraska Act, Fugitive Slave Act, Dred Scott case
    b. Fugitive Slave Act, Kansas-Nebraska Act, Dred Scott case
    c. Fugitive Slave Act, Dred Scott case, Kansas-Nebraska Act
    d. Dred Scott case, Kansas-Nebraska Act, Fugitive Slave Act

11. The Ostend Manifesto claimed Cuba as a natural part of the United States because of
    a. geographic proximity and mutual economic interests
    b. historic ties and treaty obligation
    c. the influence of the United Fruit Company
    d. all of the above

12. Which of the following statements of the southern perspective is not true?
    a. Northerners were ill-mannered, mean, and materialistic.
    b. The South was a genteel and orderly society guided by gentleman planters.
    c. Slavery was an unfortunate but necessary evil resulting from high northern tariffs.
    d. Southerners revered local self-government as a basic republican right.

13. According to the Dred Scott decision,
    a. the Compromise of 1850 was declared unconstitutional
    b. free blacks but not slaves had the right to sue in federal courts
    c. Dred Scott was entitled to his freedom because he had lived in a free state
    d. Dred Scott had no right to sue and was denied his freedom

14. Of the options facing him in the winter of 1861-1862, Lincoln favored
    a. compromising with the secessionist states
    b. letting secessionist states "go in peace"
    c. risking war by upholding the laws of the land and protecting federal property
    d. going to war in a daring first strike against the secessionist states

15. Which of the following is in the correct chronological order?
    a. John Brown's raid, secession of South Carolina, Lincoln's election, Fort Sumter
    b. Lincoln's election, secession of South Carolina, John Brown's raid, Fort Sumter
    c. John Brown's raid, Lincoln's election, secession of South Carolina, Fort Sumter
    d. Lincoln's election, John Brown's raid, secession of South Carolina, Fort Sumter

Essays

1. Explain your view of the causes of the Civil War, citing appropriate specific evidence to defend your explanation.

2. Select three or four specific events and developments in the 1850s that you think were the most significant in causing the Civil War. Defend your choices and explain why you think other events and developments were less significant.

3. Construct a dialogue between a New England migrant and a Missouri slaveholder over whether Kansas should become a slave or free state. Use your imagination in setting the scene (and the outcome), but focus your primary attention on how each person reflects his or her sectional view and how that section viewed the other.

4. Explain the reasons the majority on the Supreme Court used in deciding the *Dred Scott* v. *Sandford* case.

5. Explain why the Lincoln-Douglas debates in Illinois were significant to the outcome of the election of 1860.

Identify and Interpret: Cartoon
(that is, state who, what, where, when, and why significant)

15

The Union Severed

(1) CHAPTER OUTLINE

A young northern man, Arthur Carpenter, begs his parents for permission to join the army and wins their consent. A southern Presbyterian preacher, George Eagleton of Tennessee, feels compelled to enlist and leaves his sorrowful wife, Ethie, and their baby to go to war.

Organizing for War
    The Balance of Resources
    The Border States
    Challenges of War
    Lincoln and Davis

Clashing on the Battlefield, 1861-1862
    War in the East
    War in the West
    Naval Warfare
    Cotton Diplomacy
    Common Problems, Novel Solutions
    Political Dissension, 1862

The Tide Turns, 1863-1865
    The Emancipation Proclamation, 1863
    Unanticipated Consequences of War
    Changing Military Strategies, 1863-1865

Changes Wrought by War
    A New South
    The Victorious North
    On the Home Front, 1861-1865
    Wartime Race Relations
    Women and the War
    The Election of 1864
    Why the North Won
    The Costs of War
    Unanswered Questions

Conclusion: Union Triumphant

(2) SIGNIFICANT THEMES AND HIGHLIGHTS

1. This chapter attempts to provide a coherent picture of the Civil War as a military and diplomatic event. But, as the stories of Arthur Carpenter and the Eagletons suggest, the chapter emphasizes the impact of the war on the lives of ordinary people: soldiers who fought the war and noncombatants behind the lines, such as women like Ethie Eagleton and Emily Harris, slaves, and working-class Americans.

2. In numerous, unanticipated ways, the war transformed northern and southern society. The changes were most dramatic in the South, where by the war's end leaders were contemplating the use of slaves as soldiers, and even emancipation. Ironically, although the war was fought to save distinctly different ways of life, the conflict forced both sides to adopt similar measures and to become more alike.

3. In the North, the war was fought to save the Union. Only gradually did goals shift to include the emancipation of slaves. Lincoln's racial leadership is emphasized despite his inability to reduce racism significantly in northern society.

4. The chapter continually shows the contrasts between northern and southern resources, leadership, military strategy, wartime political and economic problems and solutions, and the impact of the war on race relations, women, daily life, and other features of the home front.

(3) LEARNING GOALS

Familiarity with Basic Knowledge

After reading this chapter, you should be able to:

1. Compare and contrast the balance of resources in the North and the South at the war's beginning and its end.

2. State the significance of the border states to both the Union and the Confederacy.

3. Explain the basic military strategies of each side.

4. List the various manpower and financial measures taken by the Confederate and Union governments during the course of the war.

5. Describe the origins, purposes, and provisions of the Emancipation Proclamation.

6. List the ways in which Lincoln and Davis expanded presidential powers.

7. Describe the participation of women and African-Americans in the war.

Practice in Historical Thinking Skills

After reading this chapter, you should be able to:

1. Discuss the social, political, and economic impact of the war on both northern and southern societies and show how the South became increasingly similar to the North.

2. Analyze the impact of the Emancipation Proclamation on the course of the war and on race relations.

3. Analyze why the North won the war and the South lost it.

(4) IMPORTANT DATES AND NAMES TO KNOW

1861	Lincoln calls up state militias and suspends habeas corpus
	First Battle of Bull Run
	Union blockades the South
1862	Battles at Shiloh, Bull Run, and Antietam
	Monitor and *Virginia* battle
	First black regiment authorized by Union
	South institutes military draft
	Union issues greenbacks
	Morrill (land-grant colleges) Act
	Pacific Railroad Act
	Homestead Act
1863	Lincoln issues Emancipation Proclamation
	Congress adopts military draft
	Battles of Gettysburg and Vicksburg
	Union Banking Act
	Southern tax laws and impressment act
	New York draft riots, Southern food riots
1864	Sherman's march through Georgia
	Lincoln reelected
	Union Banking Act
1865	Lee surrenders at Appomattox
	Lincoln assassinated
	Andrew Johnson becomes president
	Congress passes Thirteenth Amendment, abolishing slavery

Other Names to Know

General Robert E. Lee	William Seward
Henri Jomini	General Ulysses S. Grant
Jefferson Davis	Salmon Chase
General George McClellan	Horace Greeley
General William T. Sherman	General George Meade

(5) GLOSSARY OF IMPORTANT TERMS

Anaconda Plan: Union strategy to blockade South on both land and sea

cotton diplomacy: the belief in the South that cotton would generate support for the Confederate cause in Europe

bounty: the fee, ranging from $800 and $1000, paid to individuals by northern communities who wished to fill their military quota outside of their own communities

Copperheads: Northern Democrats who wished for a peaceful and speedy end to the war. The Republican press struck them with the label of the deadly snakes.

impressment: the confiscation or taking of private property for the war effort

radical: group of Republicans, never very many, who wished not only for the emancipation of the slaves but also for fundamental changes in southern society after the war

Confederacy: the name given to the new southern nation between 1861 and 1865

(6) ENRICHMENT IDEAS

1. Study a volume of photographs of the Civil War taken by Mathew Brady and others. Choose two or three photographs and study them closely. First, describe what they contain: What objects are in each? What people? How are they dressed? What are their expressions (faces and bodies)? What appears to be the relation between them? Then draw some conclusions: What atmosphere has been created? Why were the photos taken and for whom? What can you learn about the Civil War by studying photos of the conflict? What are the limitations of this kind of historical evidence? How has the technological level of the equipment shaped photography?

2. Study letters or diaries written by a participant in the Civil War. You may have some in your family, or check your college or university library archives; most historical societies will have manuscript resources of this kind. There are good printed collections of letters and diaries written by soldiers. You might also want to look at materials written by people at home. What kinds of experience does your writer

describe? What seems important to him or her? What understanding of the war does your writer have?

3. If a Civil War battlefield is nearby, visit it. Imagine yourself a typical soldier writing home with news of that battle. What would you say?

(7) SAMPLE TEST AND EXAMINATION QUESTIONS

Multiple choice: Choose the best answer.

1. Early opponents of the war included all of the following EXCEPT
   a. free blacks in the North
   b. white yeoman farmers who owned no slaves
   c. Irish immigrants
   d. northern Democrats from the Midwest

2. In 1861, Lincoln planned to increase the army by
   a. calling up state militias for three months
   b. dramatically increasing its size through bounties
   c. immediately using the draft
   d. using slaves who were offered freedom

3. In 1861, the South had the advantage of
   a. a slave population that could be recruited for the army
   b. substantial agricultural resources
   c. a larger population of males than the North
   d. an adequate railroad system

4. All of the following border states eventually joined the Confederacy EXCEPT
   a. Virginia
   b. Tennessee
   c. Kentucky
   d. Arkansas

5. In the early days of the war, Lincoln
   a. scrupulously respected individual civil rights
   b. revoked General Frémont's emancipation proclamation in Missouri
   c. ordered the immediate recruitment of black soldiers
   d. decided against a naval blockade of the South

6. The first battle of Bull Run indicated
   a. that the southern army was on the way to becoming a professional fighting force
   b. that northern commanders had a well-developed strategic plan to defeat the South
   c. that a volunteer army would be sufficient for the conflict
   d. the deficiencies of short-term enlistment

7. Cotton diplomacy failed because
   a. European powers believed the South could not win the war
   b. Europe was in a depression and could not buy cotton
   c. European industrialists found other sources of cotton
   d. European nations were not interested in the conflict

8. The war was financed on both sides mostly by
   a. government borrowing
   b. taxation
   c. foreign loans
   d. printing paper money

9. In the South,
   a. all soldiers were drafted
   b. about a third of the Confederate army was conscripted
   c. many slaves served as soldiers
   d. only slave owners served in the army

10. In the North, moderate and conservative Republicans
    a. favored the emancipation of slaves
    b. supported the use of blacks as soldiers
    c. hoped for sweeping social and economic changes in the South
    d. feared all of the above

11. The Emancipation Proclamation technically freed
    a. slaves in the border states
    b. free blacks only
    c. slaves in areas conquered by Union armies
    d. slaves in unconquered parts of the Confederacy

12. The Confederate government
    a. honored the concept of states' rights
    b. honored the principle of private property
    c. favored conscription and taxation
    d. favored using emancipated slaves as soldiers

13. The demands of war produced
    a. deflation
    b. inflation
    c. increases in real wages
    d. heavy unemployment

14. Grant's final campaign
    a. was intended to secure the Mississippi River
    b. was aimed at luring Lee into one final, decisive battle
    c. was aimed at the total destruction of all Confederate armies and resources
    d. depended on guerrilla warfare

15. The Civil War
    a. was a tremendous boon to northern industry
    b. stimulated northern manufacturing only in certain war-related industries
    c. had surprisingly little effect on industry
    d. created financial chaos and thus disrupted industry

Identify and show a relationship between each of the following pairs:

Emily Harris	*and*	Arthur Carpenter
Emancipation Proclamation	*and*	Antietam
Jefferson Davis	*and*	Greenbacks
General William Sherman	*and*	"total war"

Essays

1. Think about and write essays on items 1-3 found in "Learning Goals" in the section "Practice in Historical Thinking Skills."

2. "If one is to understand the Civil War, it is important to realize that it was not fought to end slavery." Develop an essay showing the extent to which you agree or disagree with this statement.

3. "Lincoln's masterful leadership was the main ingredient of northern victory." To what extent do you agree or disagree with this statement?

Identify and Interpret: Quotation
(that is, state who, what, where, when, and why significant)

With malice toward none; with charity for all; with firmness in the right, as God gives us to see the right, let us strive on to finish the work we are in; to bind up the nation's wounds; to care for him who shall have borne the battle, and for his widow, and his orphan—to do all which may achieve and cherish a just, and a lasting peace, among ourselves, and with all nations.

Map Question

Locate the following on the accompanying map.

1. Washington, D.C.
2. the eleven Confederate States of America
3. Fort Sumter
4. Antietam and Bull Run
5. Shiloh
6. Vicksburg
7. Mississippi River
8. Gettysburg
9. Sherman's route to the sea
10. Montgomery, Alabama
11. the four border states remaining in the Union
12. Appomattox
13. new state seceding from Virginia, 1863
14. Ohio River

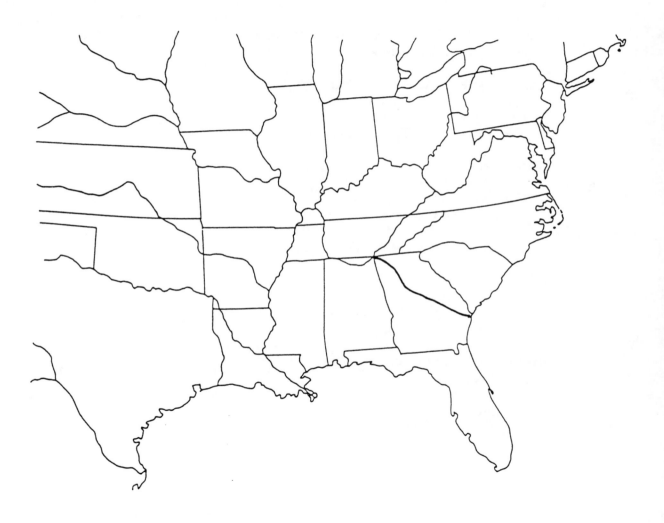

16

The Union Reconstructed

(1) CHAPTER OUTLINE

Adele and Elizabeth Allston fearfully return to their plantations after the war. At Nightingale Hall, they have a joyous reunion with their former slaves. But at Guendalos, the blacks are defiant, the atmosphere threatening. The morning after the arrival, however, Uncle Jacob, the former black driver, hands the keys to the crop barns over to the women in recognition that they still own the land.

The Bittersweet Aftermath of War
    The United States in 1865
    Hopes Among Freedmen
    The White South's Fearful Response

National Reconstruction
    The Presidential Plan
    Congressional Reconstruction
    The President Impeached
    Congressional Moderation
    Women and the Reconstruction Amendments

Life After Slavery
    The Freedmen's Bureau
    Economic Freedom by Degrees
    Black Self-Help Institutions

Reconstruction in the States
    Republican Rule
    Violence and "Redemption"
    Reconstruction, Northern Style
    The End of Reconstruction

Conclusion: A Mixed Legacy

(2) SIGNIFICANT THEMES AND HIGHLIGHTS

1. The account of the Allstons' return to their plantations highlights the focus of this chapter. The primary action of the chapter takes place on the old southern plantation

and in the freedmen's cabins, not in the halls of Congress and the White House. Rather than emphasizing the political programs and conflicts of Congress and the president, we see the hopes and fears of ordinary persons—both black and white—as they faced their postwar world. Political events, North as well as South in the years between 1865 and 1877, are included, but they are secondary to the psychosocial dynamics of reconstructing new relationships among differing people after the Civil War.

2. As reflected in the opening anecdote, the dreams and aspirations of three groups—white southerners, black freedmen, and white northerners—are introduced and woven together throughout the chapter. The main question of the chapter is, What happens as these three sets of goals come into conflict? Uncle Jacob's return of the keys to the crop barns to the Allston family, a gesture symbolic of ownership, indicates the crucial importance of labor and land to an understanding of the outcome of these conflicting goals. The result was a mixed legacy of human gains and losses.

3. The experiences of the Allston family are concluded in this chapter. Frederick Douglass's astute observations as a black leader continue as those of W. E. B. Du Bois begin.

4. The tragic elements of the Reconstruction, or any other era, are perhaps best represented in literature. Novels and short stories are used in this chapter to capture these human conflicts.

(3) LEARNING GOALS

Familiarity with Basic Knowledge

After reading this chapter, you should be able to:

1. State four or five particular goals of three groups at the end of the Civil War: the freedmen, white southerners, and white northerners.

2. Describe the situation and mood of the country at the end of the Civil War and describe the first programs and actions of southern whites and freedmen as they redefined race relations in 1865.

3. Explain President Johnson's reconstruction program and contrast it with Congress's alternative program.

4. Name and explain three important acts and three constitutional amendments that were part of the Republican reconstruction program.

5. Explain the arrangements for working the land that developed between white landowners and the freedmen and describe the terms of a typical work contract.

6. Describe the character of the Republican state governments in the South during Reconstruction: Who ruled? How well? For how long? How did these governments come to an end?

7. Explain how Reconstruction ended.

Practice in Historical Thinking Skills

After reading this chapter, you should be able to:

1. Assess the relationship between the character of national politics during Grant's term of office from 1869 to 1877 and the end of Reconstruction in the South.

2. Show how the diverse goals of the white southerners, freedmen, and white northerners came into conflict and assess to what extent each group achieved its various goals by the end of Reconstruction.

3. Evaluate the respective roles southern and northern whites played in impeding black goals.

(4) IMPORTANT DATES AND NAMES TO KNOW

1865	Civil War ends
	Lincoln assassinated; Andrew Johnson becomes president
	Johnson's general amnesty and reconstruction plan
	Racial confusion, widespread hunger, and demobilization
	Thirteenth Amendment ratified (abolishing slavery)
	Freedmen's Bureau established
1865-1866	Black codes passed throughout ex-Confederate states
	Repossession of land by whites and signing of contracts with freedmen
1866	Freedmen's Bureau bill renewed over Johnson's veto
	Civil Rights Act passed over Johnson's veto
	Southern Homestead Act
	Ku Klux Klan formed
	Tennessee readmitted to Union
1867	Reconstruction Acts passed over Johnson's veto
	Impeachment controversy
	Freedmen's Bureau ends
1868	Impeachment trial of Johnson fails
	Ulysses S. Grant elected president
	Fourteenth Amendment ratified
1868-1870	Readmission of ten states under congressional plan

1869	Georgia and Virginia reestablish Democratic party control
1870	Fifteenth Amendment ratified
1870-1871	Force and Ku Klux Klan acts passed by Congress North Carolina and Georgia reestablish Democratic control
1870s-1880s	Black "exodusters" migrate to Kansas
1872	General Amnesty Act Grant reelected president
1873	Texas reestablishes Democratic party control Crédit Mobilier scandal Panic causes depression
1874	Alabama and Arkansas reestablish Democratic party control
1875	Civil Rights Act Mississippi Plan reestablishes Democratic control
1876	Disputed Hayes-Tilden election
1876-1877	South Carolina, Louisiana, and Florida reestablish Democratic party control
1877	Compromise of 1877 Rutherford B. Hayes assumes presidency and ends Reconstruction
1880s	Tenancy and sharecropping prevail in the South Disfranchisement and segregation of southern blacks begins

Other Names to Know

Edwin Stanton
Susan B. Anthony
Frederick Douglass
W. E. B. Du Bois

Jay Gould
Charles Sumner
Benjamin "Pap" Singleton

General O. O. Howard
Thaddeus Stevens
Elizabeth Cady Stanton

(5) GLOSSARY OF IMPORTANT TERMS

freedmen: former slaves emancipated by the Thirteenth Amendment

carpetbagger: a derogatory term applied to northerners who settled in the South after the Civil War

scalawag: a derogatory term applied to southern Unionists who supported Republican state governments during Reconstruction

debt slavery/peonage: the economic situation in which tenant farmers or sharecroppers become trapped in perpetual debt because they always owe more to their landlords than they get from the sale of cotton or other crops

amnesty: removing blame and punishment for past crimes

radical Republicans: a derogatory term applied to northern Republican politicians who generally wanted not only to punish the ex-Confederate leaders but also to help the freedmen fulfill their goals (overstated term; most Republicans were moderate)

"waving the bloody shirt": a Republican political campaign tactic of reminding voters of the Civil War and the valuable role of the Republican party in preserving the Union and defeating the rebellious (Democratic) South

exodusters: disillusioned blacks who fled the South in the 1870s and 1880s to settle in all-black towns in the western prairies

redemption: a word used by southerners to describe the return of conservative Democrats to power in southern state governments, thus removing the so-called radical Republicans from power

Grantism: a term describing political corruption and graft in the North in the 1870s

(6) ENRICHMENT IDEAS

1. The Recovering the Past section, which focuses on the ways in which novels reflect history, includes only a very brief excerpt from two novels about Reconstruction. Consider in a longer excerpt the style and point of view of the authors of the six novels listed below. Which do you think most accurately reflects the historical truth about Reconstruction? Is the most accurate novel-as-history necessarily the best as literature? Based on these excerpts, which novel do you think you would like to read in its entirety and why?

   Thomas Dixon, Jr., *The Clansman*
   Albion Tourgée, *A Fool's Errand*
   Howard Fast, *Freedom Road*
   W. E. B. Du Bois, *Quest of the Silver Fleece*
   John DeForest, *Miss Ravenal's Conversion from Secession to Loyalty*
   Earnest Gaines, *The Autobiography of Miss Jane Pittman*

2. Complete the textbook chart "Conflicting Goals During Reconstruction" for the following groups in 1865 by showing what happened to each group by 1877. How well were each of their earlier goals fulfilled? When you have completed the chart,

you are in a position to assess the success of Reconstruction and to understand developments in the South into the twentieth century.

    a. victorious northern radical Republicans
    b. northern moderates - Republicans and Democrats
    c. old southern planter aristocracy (ex-Confederates)
    d. New "Other South" yeoman farmers and Unionists
    e. black freedmen

3. Write a short story or a series of letters or diary entries describing the typical daily experiences of various persons during Reconstruction. For example, a southern woman, Adele Allston, or her daughter Elizabeth, presiding over a large cotton plantation in the absence of their husband and father who was killed in the war. Or a black family that had been given 40 acres of confiscated land by a northern general during the war and faced a title dispute with and dispossession by the original landowner afterwards. Or a poor white family putting its life together in the changing economic climate and race relationships of the postwar years. Or a Yankee schoolteacher's experiences in a Freedmen's Bureau school in Tennessee. Or a Freedmen's Bureau agent's hectic, overworked, underappreciated daily duties in Mississippi. Read in class and discuss. Notice the clash of unresolved dreams.

(7) SAMPLE TEST AND EXAMINATION QUESTIONS

Multiple choice: Choose the best answer.

1.   Which of the following is in the correct order?
    a. Black codes, Fourteenth Amendment, Mississippi Plan
    b. Fourteenth Amendment, Mississippi Plan, Reconstruction Acts
    c. Black codes, Mississippi Plan, Fourteenth Amendment
    d. Mississippi Plan, Black codes, Reconstruction Acts

2.   All of the following are true descriptions of the United States in April 1865 EXCEPT
    a. many southern cities were physically devastated
    b. black ex-slaves were in a confused state of semifreedom
    c. the defeated southern rebels were eager to regain their former lands and laborers
    d. most northerners wanted to punish the southern rebels severely

3.   Which one is *not* true of the freedmen in the first months of emancipation?
    a. they went searching for missing family members
    b. they left the plantation briefly but usually returned to the place and work they knew best
    c. they showed great interest in getting an education
    d. they left their masters as soon as possible, usually stealing property as an expression of revenge

4. Congressional Republicans passed all of the following bills EXCEPT
   a. a land bill granting 40 acres and a mule to black Union veterans
   b. a civil rights bill
   c. Reconstruction acts dividing the South into five military districts
   d. a bill extending the Freedmen's Bureau

5. The heart of President Johnson's Reconstruction program was
   a. to punish all wealthy ex-Confederates by confiscating their land
   b. general amnesty and pardons for most ex-Confederates
   c. insistence on passage of the Fourteenth Amendment
   d. a land bill for poor and middle-class southern whites

6. The most obvious failure of the Freedmen's Bureau was in its role
   a. distributing emergency rations
   b. setting the freedmen up on their own land
   c. setting up schools for the freedmen
   d. facilitating family reunions and marriage and work for the freedmen

7. Most Republican politicians in the Reconstruction era were motivated by all of the following EXCEPT
   a. the desire to maintain political power
   b. some idealistic concern for protecting the civil rights of the freedmen
   c. a vindictive desire to confiscate rebel land and redistribute it among blacks
   d. a concern for securing the continued economic growth of northern industry

8. Republican state governments in the South were
   a. dominated by blacks
   b. dominated by "carpetbaggers" and "scalawags"
   c. hampered by the fact that federal troops left the South so quickly
   d. the most corrupt in the nation

9. State governments in the South during Reconstruction accomplished all of the following EXCEPT
   a. providing public school systems
   b. approving generous measures for economic rebuilding
   c. liberalizing divorce and penal laws
   d. guaranteeing permanent black suffrage

10. The Democrats returned to power in the South because
    a. the Republicans made such a mess of the tax system
    b. blacks did not receive 40 acres and a mule
    c. secret organizations used violence to drive out Republicans
    d. Grant realized that the Republican party was harming itself by its policies on the state level

11. By the 1870s, the Republican party
    a. was reinforced as the party of moral reform and black rights
    b. became more and more a party representing big business
    c. blocked most transportation schemes
    d. supported women's rights

12. Grant's administration was characterized by
    a. scandals like the Whiskey Ring affair
    b. an excess of democracy
    c. zealous attempts to reduce graft
    d. none of the above

13. The Civil Rights Act of 1875
    a. condemned the Ku Klux Klan for violations of the Fourteenth Amendment
    b. passed the House but was defeated in the Senate
    c. passed both houses of Congress but was vetoed by the president
    d. was passed by Congress and signed by the president but not really enforced

14. The significance of the election of 1877 was that it
    a. ended Reconstruction
    b. resulted in the removal of the last federal troops from the South
    c. resulted in federal aid for the South
    d. all of the above

15. Which best summarizes the nation in 1877?
    a. Reconstruction had fulfilled the dreams of the freedmen
    b. the white South had won everything during Reconstruction that they had lost during the war
    c. concern for rights and condition of the freedmen was no longer a major priority
    d. women were the real winners of Reconstruction because they could now vote

Briefly identify and show a relationship between each of the following pairs.

General O. O. Howard	*and*	Thaddeus Stevens
Black codes	*and*	the Fourteenth Amendment
proclamation of general amnesty	*and*	the Reconstruction Acts
freedmen work contracts	*and*	southern homestead acts
Mississippi Plan of 1875	*and*	Force Act of 1870-1871
"40 acres and a mule"	*and*	"peace at any price"
annual wage contract	*and*	sharecropping

Essays

1. Use items 1-3 under "Practice in Historical Thinking Skills" in the "Learning Goals" section to develop essays.

2. In *The Souls of Black Folk,* W. E. B. Du Bois wrote: "So the Freedmen's Bureau died, and its child was the Fifteenth Amendment." Discuss, showing how this statement might be interpreted as an apt summary of Reconstruction.

3. In *The Souls of Black Folk,* W. E. B. Du Bois says: "Negro suffrage ended a civil war by beginning a race feud." Discuss the heritage of Reconstruction. To what extent did the events of that period create a continuing race feud in America, sectional animosity, and patterns of political party allegiance? To what extent do these phenomena still exist? How would you have done better?

ANSWERS TO SAMPLE TEST AND EXAMINATION QUESTIONS*

Chapter 1	Chapter 2	Chapter 3	Chapter 4	Chapter 5
1. a	1. c	1. b	1. a	1. c
2. d	2. b	2. c	2. d	2. a
3. b	3. a	3. d	3. c	3. d
4. b	4. a	4. a	4. d	4. a
5. d	5. b	5. d	5. d	5. b
6. c	6. c	6. a	6. c	6. c
7. d	7. b	7. b	7. c	7. c
8. b	8. d	8. b	8. c	8. b
9. c	9. a	9. b	9. d	9. c
10. a	10. d	10. c	10. a	10. b
11. c	11. c	11. d	11. b	11. d
12. c	12. c	12. d	12. c	12. c
13. c	13. a	13. d	13. d	13. b
14. d	14. d	14. c	14. b	14. d
15. a	15. c	15. a	15. d	15. a
			16. a	

Chapter 6

Multiple Choice

1. a
2. b
3. b
4. a
5. c
6. d
7. c
8. a
9. b
10. b
11. d
12. c
13. d
14. c

Order & Dates

1. 1763 End of Seven Years' War
2. 1765 Stamp Act
3. 1773 Boston Tea Party
4. 1775 Lexington and Concord
5. 1776 Declaration of Independence
6. 1777 Battle of Saratoga
7. 1781 Yorktown
8. 1783 Treaty of Paris
9. 1784 Treaty of Fort Stanwix
10. 1787 Constitutional Convention

Answers to the Quotation and Chart Identifications and the Map Questions are found at the end of this section.

Chapter 7		Chapter 8	Chapter 9
Multiple Choice	**True/False**		
1. a	1. True	1. c	1. c
2. b	2. False	2. b	2. c
3. d	3. True	3. b	3. b
4. d	4. True	4. c	4. a
5. a	5. False	5. a	5. b
6. c	6. True	6. c	6. d
7. d	7. False	7. d	7. a
8. c	8. True	8. a	8. b
9. a	9. False	9. b	9. c
10. c	10. True	10. d	10. b
11. d	11. True	11. a	11. b
12. a	12. True	12. b	12. a
13. b	13. False	13. c	13. d
	14. False		14. a
	15. False		15. d
	16. True		
	17. False		
	18. False		

Chapter 10	Chapter 11	Chapter 12		Chapter 13
		Multiple Choice	**Matching**	
1. d	1. c	1. c	1. e	1. d
2. b	2. d	2. b	2. l	2. d
3. b	3. a	3. d	3. a	3. b
4. c	4. a	4. b	4. f	4. a
5. d	5. b	5. b	5. j	5. c
6. b	6. a	6. c	6. i	6. d
7. d	7. a	7. b	7. n	7. c
8. a	8. c	8. c	8. c	8. b
9. c	9. b	9. b	9. m	9. b
10. c	10. c	10. b	10. o	10. c
11. b	11. c	11. a	11. b	11. c
12. d	12. b	12. d	12. h	12. d
13. c	13. b	13. b	13. d	13. b
14. c	14. b	14. d	14. k	14. c
15. b	15. c	15. b	15. g	15. d
16. a	16. c			
17. c				

Chapter 14
Multiple Choice

1. a
2. c
3. c
4. b
5. d
6. a
7. d
8. a
9. b
10. b
11. a
12. c
13. d
14. c
15. c

Chapter 15

1. a
2. a
3. b
4. c
5. b
6. d
7. c
8. d
9. b
10. d
11. d
12. c
13. b
14. c
15. b

Chapter 16

1. a
2. d
3. d
4. a
5. b
6. b
7. c
8. c
9. d
10. c
11. b
12. a
13. d
14. d
15. c

ANSWERS: IDENTIFY AND INTERPRET

Chapter 2 - Quotation

John Winthrop, "A Model of Christian Charity," a sermon delivered on board the *Arbella* while crossing the Atlantic in 1630. A statement of the importance of a covenant, both among the Puritans and with God, in establishing a model community of saints for others to admire and imitate.

Chapter 3 - Chart: Colonial Population

1. This chart highlights the growth of white and black population between 1640 and 1770. At the beginning of the period, blacks constituted only a tiny portion of the country's people, but by 1770 they made up 21% of the population. The chart shows that over the period as a whole the black population grew proportionately faster than the white.

2. Some of the reasons explaining white population growth include large family size, relatively healthy living conditions, ample diet, and, not the least, continuing migration from Europe. Black population increase resulted from the gradual formation of black families and the escalation of the slave trade (which, in turn, was triggered by the declining supply of indentured servants in the late seventeenth century and the continuing need for labor in the colonies).

3. The chart illustrates the peopling of the new world and the increasing opportunity for the emergence of an American culture as more settlers of each race put down roots. The chart also makes clear the colonies' increasing reliance on slavery and highlights the important role slaves played in the American economy.

Chapter 4 - Quotation

Jonathan Edwards, "Sinners in the Hand of an Angry God," Enfield, Connecticut, 1741. One of the most famous and powerful sermons during the Great Awakening.

Chapter 6 - Quotation

Abigail Adams, letter to husband John Adams, 1776, as he is preparing to sign the Declaration of Independence. An early feminist reminder that revolutionary "natural" rights in America were for white men only and that women would use familiar arguments in achieving their liberation.

Chapter 7 - Quotation

Anti-Federalist (Patrick Henry) argument against ratification of the Constitution, Virginia, 1788. In a debate with James Madison, Henry states the classic case that the states, not the people, formed the compact creating the new government. The argument would be reiterated until the Civil War settled the issues.

Chapter 8 - Quotation

Two pronouncements from gatherings of Democratic-Republican artisan groups in 1795: the first is a 4th of July festival supporting Tom Paine's defense of French revolutionary principle against British conservatism; the second a toast at a New York Juvenile Republican Society dinner. Both show the democratic attitude of workers, drawn more and more into the politics of the 1790s.

Chapter 9 - Quotation

Thomas Jefferson, Inaugural Address, 1801. Although seeking reconciliation with the Federalists, Jefferson articulates the Republican program of expansion ("with room enough. . .", limited government, equality of opportunity, and religious and economic freedom.

Chapter 10 - Quotation

Regulations from a New England boarding house for women workers in the mills, from the 1820s or 1830s. The rules were an attempt to ensure that women workers lived in a respectable manner and had enough sleep to work efficiently. The regulations highlight the regimentation of life in a mill town but also hint at the sense of sisterhood which these boarding house arrangements often fostered.

Chapter 12 - Quotation

Declaration of Sentiments, Women's Rights Convention, Seneca Falls, New York, 1848. Drafted by Elizabeth Cady Stanton, and modeled on the Declaration of Independence, the Seneca Falls Declaration and resolutions signaled the women's rights agenda for the century to follow.

Chapter 12 - Chart: Public Land Sales, 1820-1860

1. The chart illustrates the pattern of public land sales between 1820 and 1860. The decades of the 1830s and the 1850s saw spectacular increases in the sale of public lands, followed by sharp declines. Note the Panic of 1837 and subsequent depression.

2. Some of the factors which contributed to the patterns apparent here include the opening of new territories for settlement, legislation which made it easier and cheaper for Americans to acquire land, improvements in transportation and the growth of markets which made settlement attractive, land hunger on the part of both free farmers and slaveholders, large scale speculation, and easy banking policies.

3. The chart as a whole suggests the expansion of agriculture (and of settlers) into new western lands, the displacement of Native Americans, the impact of feverish speculation on the economy, and the periods of economic expansion in the 1830s and 1850s with the sharp contractions which followed.

Chapter 14 - Cartoon

A Know-Nothing (American Party) cartoon stereotyping the new Irish and German immigrants of the early 1850s as whiskey and beer-drinking ruffians who steal off with the ballot box (presumably to a saloon).

Chapter 15 - Quotation

Abraham Lincoln, Second Inaugural Address, 1865. Delivered less than six weeks before his assassination, the second inaugural is one of the most eloquent and stirring presidential addresses in American history.

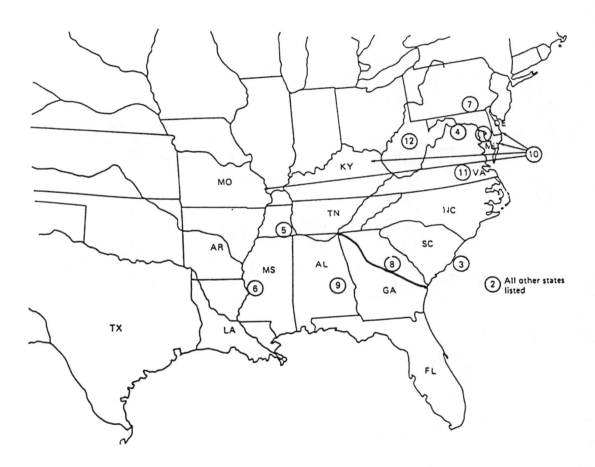